The Rescue of Romanticism

The Rescue *of* Romanticism

WALTER PATER AND JOHN RUSKIN

❧ Kenneth Daley

Ohio University Press
Athens

Ohio University Press, Athens, Ohio 45701
© 2001 by Kenneth Daley
Printed in the United States of America
All rights reserved

Ohio University Press books are printed on acid-free paper ∞™

09 08 07 06 05 04 03 02 01 5 4 3 2 1

LIBRARY OF CONGRESS CATALOGING-IN-PUBLICATION DATA
Daley, Kenneth, 1962–
    The rescue of Romanticism : Walter Pater and John Ruskin / Kenneth
    Daley.
    p. cm.
    Includes bibliographical references and index.
    ISBN 0-8214-1382-1
    1. Pater, Walter, 1839–1894—Criticism and interpretation. 2. English
    literature—19th century—History and criticism. 3. Ruskin, John,
    1819–1900—Criticism and interpretation. 4. Art criticism—Great
    Britain—History—19th century. 5. Romanticism—Great Britain. I.
    Title.

PR5137 .D35 2001
824'.8—dc21

                                            2001016308

For Devorah,

for everything

Contents

Illustrations

Acknowledgments

This study began, long ago, as a dissertation under the direction of Harold Bloom. As a graduate student, I felt strongly the allure of Bloom's own writing on Pater and Ruskin, and I am grateful for his advice and encouragement. My thanks also to Perry Meisel for his generous support throughout my graduate and professional careers. I have benefited enormously from his comments on my manuscript, both in its early form and as it grew into a book. John Maynard, Jennifer Wagner-Lawlor, Susan Crowl, Billie Andrew Inman, Allan Dooley, Martin Danahay, and Peter Erb have each read all or part of the manuscript and offered valuable criticisms and suggestions. I am grateful for their intellectual generosity.

My colleagues in the Ohio University English department have been sympathetic supporters and friends. I wish especially to thank Susan and Samuel Crowl for being inexhaustible sources of sage counsel and high spirit. My former chair, Betty Pytlik, helped secure a course reduction during a particularly difficult period of writing. Bob Miklitsch and Tom Scanlan gave me excellent advice at a crucial moment. I also wish to thank Leslie Fleming, Dean of the College of Arts and Sciences, and Roger Rollins, Associate Dean of Research, for covering the expenses of the book's illustrations.

I am grateful to the participants and organizers of the following professional meetings for giving me the opportunity to present my work-in-progress: the International Conference on John Ruskin at the Armstrong Browning Library, the Conference on Beauty in the

Nineteenth Century at the University of Toronto, the Romantic and Victorian section of the 1997 SAMLA, the 1998 Victorians' Institute Conference, and the Art of Ruskin seminar at the 2000 ACLA.

At the Ohio University Press, thanks to David Sanders for backing my manuscript and watching over its transformation into a book. Thanks also to Nancy Basmajian and Beth Pratt for their work in the editorial and production process, and Evan Young for his expert copyediting.

A brief section of chapter 1 appeared in *Victorian Newsletter* (Spring 1998) as part of my essay "Figures of Restraint: The Ruskinian Gentleman and the Romantic Artist." A section of chapter 3 appeared in *Prose Studies* (August 1997) as a section of "From the Theoretic to the Practical: Ruskin, British Aestheticism, and the Relation of Art to Use."

My deepest gratitude goes to Raphael Falco, who has lived with this book as long as I have and finally commanded that it be finished. His ideas and expressions have been so freely appropriated that it is impossible to indicate the extent of my debt.

Thanks also to Ani Proser, Fred Eisenberg, Leslie Goehl, Sam Crowl, David Lazar, and Mark Halliday, for support and friendly encouragement. The support of my mother and father, Rhoda Daley and Marvin Daley, and the rest of my family extends far beyond friendship—thanks to Carole Daley, my sister Debra DeCosta and her husband Joseph, my in-laws Mimi and Larry Silberstein, and Avi, Uri and Jackie, Rachel and Hussein.

Finally, I acknowledge my most profound blessings, my two boys, Charlie and Leo, and my wife, to whom this book is dedicated.

The Rescue of Romanticism

Introduction ❧ The Rescue of
Romanticism

W ALTER PATER'S early biographer, A. C. Benson, reports
that Pater used to pretend that he shut his eyes when
crossing the Alps so as not to see those "horrid pots of blue
paint," his standard epithet for the Swiss lakes (191). In sharp contrast
to the other great romantic critic of the later nineteenth century, John
Ruskin, whose life and career were so intimately connected to the
Alps, Pater was uninterested in the close observation of rocks or
stones or trees or clouds or waves. He never went climbing. Pater's vision of the natural world is almost always a mediated one, derived not
from time spent in the field but from time spent in the study contem-
plating the varied representations of nature in poetry and painting, in
myth and philosophy and history, in chemistry and biology and the
developing sciences of anthropology and archaeology. Ruskin depended on an immediate and close interaction with the natural world,
the visible correspondence to the revealed word of the Bible. His
"blessed entrance into life," he writes in *Praeterita*, came at the moment
he first beheld the glory of the Alps from Schaffhausen, a moment of
consecration revealing not only "the beauty of the earth, but the open-
ing of the first page of its volume" (35:115–16).[1] There is no theophanic

vision on the mountaintop for Pater, no mystical communion with Nature. In the words of Wendell V. Harris, "the great importance of Pater for late nineteenth-century literary and intellectual history lies in the wholeheartedness with which he bids farewell to transcendentalism" (*Omnipresent Debate*, 346).

Pater's farewell to transcendentalism constitutes a crucial foundation of modernist (and postmodernist) literature and aesthetics. As scholars have demonstrated, Pater is a pervasive presence in twentieth-century literature and theory.[2] But while his legacy has attracted a great deal of critical attention, his intellectual origins, especially in the eighteenth and nineteenth centuries, have been somewhat neglected.[3] The present study helps to address this critical gap by establishing and defining Pater's relation to his older contemporary Ruskin. While critics have always acknowledged Pater's dependence on Ruskin, there has never been a study detailing their intertextual relationship.

This book focuses on Pater and Ruskin as theorists of romanticism. I read Pater's theory of romantic art as a response to Ruskin's more ambivalent theory that regards the modern period as a perversion of the romantic ideal. My aim throughout is to distinguish the rhetorical manipulations through which Pater resists what he perceives to be Ruskin's conservative approach, which associates modern romantic art with antinomianism, faithlessness, and social anarchy.[4] In his response to Ruskin, Pater establishes the nature of romanticism as a site of intense political and cultural debate.

Pater scholars have related Pater's idea of romanticism to Platonic and Hegelian notions of palingenesis, metempsychosis, and the anthropological notion of survival that derives from Edward Tylor (Shuter, "History as Palingenesis"; Crawford; Inman, "Pater and His Reading"). These terms, descriptive of Pater's various mythifications, help us to focus the very distinctions between continuity and discontinuity in historical narrative with which Pater is most concerned in his responses to Ruskin. I think that in the final analysis both Pater and Ruskin are most concerned with versions of continuity. Ruskin, being more of a cultural alarmist, often calls attention to precipitous discontinuities in his jeremiads against the decay of modern culture. But it would be mistaken to conclude that by extension he does not believe in continuity. In fact, Ruskin's zealous program of social reform stands as proof of his conviction not only in the possibility of continuity but also in his own ability to help inspire it.

In contrast to Ruskin, Pater wears his belief in continuity on his sleeve. He insists on seeing a continuity of the romantic spirit despite apparent conflicts in the myths and means of expression through which that spirit has been manifest from epoch to historical epoch. Ruskin too has a theory of the romantic spirit, although he believes that its revival in the modern era is vexed. That Pater's and Ruskin's definitions of the romantic spirit often seem to clash, however, does not diminish their comparable commitment to the romantic ideal.

Romanticism has been a much contested category ever since the word emerged as a technical term in eighteenth-century Europe. The confusion of terminology and thought is so acute that in our time it has come to epitomize the problem of literary history itself, calling into question the logic and procedures of periodization and literary classification (Perkins; Lindenberger; Siskin; Arac). Theorists of romanticism have long faced the conceptual problems that Ihab Hassan has recently identified with the problem of postmodernism, including its semantic and historical instability, its simultaneously synchronic and diachronic nature, and its contradictory character, which demands a "dialectical vision, for defining traits are often antithetical" (150).[5] Not surprisingly, contemporary scholars are especially apt to perceive romanticism not as a coherent or unified phenomenon, but as a "site of questioning," of variation and fragmentation (Beer, 248; Butler).[6] One recent theorist approaches romanticism via chaos theory, characterizing the romantic phenomenon as a "loose species of machinic organisms" or "ideologemes" that thrive on ambivalence and contradiction (Livingston, 12). In another recent attempt to account for romanticism's "extraordinarily contradictory character," Robert Sayre and Michael Lowy describe the term as a *coincidentia oppositorum*" and outline a number of its prevalent antitheses: "revolutionary

and counterrevolutionary, cosmopolitan and nationalist, realist and
fanciful, restorationist and utopian, democratic and aristocratic, re-
publican and monarchist, red and white, mystical and sensual" (24).[7]
The competing theories of Pater and Ruskin prefigure many of
these contradictions that characterize the Anglo-American reception
of romanticism in the twentieth century. As two of the first aesthetic
philosophers in England to theorize "romanticism," their conflicting
ideas provide a structure by means of which to consider subsequent
evaluations of the term including the most conspicuous modern
disagreements—the New Humanist and New Critical indictment of
romanticism and the response of their antagonists as well as the more
recent post-Althusserian Marxist opposition to the idealist tradition
of romantic criticism. Unlike their counterparts on the continent,
English writers of the first half of the nineteenth century never referred to their own contemporary literature as "romantic," and the
Schlegels' famous classical-romantic distinction, although well known
in England particularly after the 1813 publication in English of
Madame de Staël's D'Allemagne, never inspired the fierce debates that
it did in Germany, France, Italy, and Spain.[8] The rise of the idea of romanticism in England, as John Beer writes, "was gradual, heuristic,
even haphazard," and it is still not adequately understood (244). Literary historians are particularly unclear about the significance of the
term in Victorian England. In what is still the most substantial history of the development of the term "romanticism" in England, George
Whalley describes the second half of the nineteenth century as a "dead
zone where navigation is difficult," where conclusions can only "be in-
ferred, largely from negative evidence" (235, 244). One of the aims of
the present study, therefore, is to give a more detailed picture of romanticism's emergence as a literary concept in England in the second
half of the nineteenth century.

Beginning with Francis Jeffrey's 1802 account of the "Lake Poets" as
a sect of "dissenters," the romantic movement was consistently associated in England with a libertarian repudiation of moral law (Perkins,
85–120). Pater is the first English writer to use the word "romantic"
while defending what he calls the "romantic tendencies" of modern lit-

erature. Critics have been slow to acknowledge this role, even though Pater's reputation as a purveyor of what Harold Bloom describes as a "de-idealized" romanticism has received a good deal of attention.[9]

The contemptuous characterization of the English romantic movement was given its most vigorous expression by the Victorian critic, W. J. Courthope, for whom "the modern romantic school" reflects an unhealthy "unbounded liberty of the imagination," promoting "egotism" and a disregard for "civic life" ("Wordsworth and Gray," 56, 60).[10] In its "sentimental desire for lawless and primitive freedom," romanticism is the enemy of both culture and civilization (Courthope, "English Poetry," 36). To the conservative critics led by Courthope, Pater's writing most clearly exemplifies what they conceive to be the major defects of romanticism: excessive subjectivism, obscure subject matter, indefinite thought, and a perverse preoccupation with style (R. V. Johnson, 42–57). Courthope writes in his 1876 essay "Wordsworth and Gray" that Pater is "the most thoroughly representative critic that the romantic school has yet produced," and after quoting from the "Conclusion" to *The Renaissance* he reflects upon the activity of a poetic imagination inspired by Pater's words.

> [I]t sets itself to stimulate . . . speculation on those questions lying at the very foundation of society. . . . It throws new and attractive colours over doubts on religion; it presents in an imaginative form a subtle casuistry about matters of morality, which the unsophisticated conscience had been accustomed to decide off-hand. Above all, it delights to handle in a thousand forms problems relating to the passion of so-called love. Love, as it is represented in modern poetry, is no longer the noble and chivalrous devotion of old romance . . . but an epicene something between a physical impulse and an intellectual curiosity, a caricature of the Eros of the Greek mystics. (69–70)

Courthope seizes on the antinomian element in Pater's prose because he believes Pater is the proponent of a radical liberalism that, from his point of view, seriously threatens the foundations of English society, including the traditional sanctities of religion, morality, and sexual love.

Recent scholars seem to agree with Courthope, but they are happy about it. They argue that Pater radicalizes Victorian liberal assumptions, especially inasmuch as he tries to establish homosexuality as a positive social identity (Dowling, *Hellenism*; Dellamora, *Masculine Desire*; Morgan, "Reimagining Masculinity"). It is reasonable to see Pater's defense of romanticism as analogous to his radicalizing of Victorian social identity. Even his insistence on what Laurel Brake describes as "a classicism which itself contains important strains of romanticism" ("After Studies," 116) reflects this radicalizing impulse. Pater's writings on romanticism complement the homosexual "counterdiscourse" of Oxford Hellenism.[11] In his conception of the romantic spirit, Pater stands as the first cultural critic in England to advocate the sociopolitical benefits of romantic art and philosophy. Throughout his career and well into our own century, Pater has stood in direct opposition to critics who perceive romanticism to be a destructive movement promoting individual desire and liberty.

While Pater's defense of romanticism answers Victorian cultural critics like Courthope, his terms and themes derive primarily from his reading of Ruskin. In 1858, at the age of nineteen, Pater first read Ruskin, the one great, unavoidable presence in nineteenth-century England for any person interested in art criticism and aesthetic theory. For Pater he was also a spectacular model of the critic as artist. His exhilarating, overwhelming, emotionally versatile style could never be Pater's, but Ruskin revealed the immense expressive potential of critical prose.[12] Furthermore, Pater recognized in Ruskin a set of critical interests closely resembling his own.

In Ruskin, Pater found the familiar Tory critique of romantic liberty, but from the pen of the writer who, in his vision of Gothic architecture, had most famously linked the romantic ideal to an endorsement of liberal values. "The Nature of Gothic" presents to its mid-Victorian readers Ruskin's idealization of the romantic spirit as a remedy for the ills of nineteenth-century England's laissez-faire eco-

nomic system and its degradation of the industrial laborer. As Linda
Dowling has recently remarked, however, "The Nature of Gothic"
represents "the window of aesthetic liberalism in Ruskin's career" (*Vulgarization of Art*, 27). The window would never again be so wide open.
Already in *The Stones of Venice* Ruskin's liberal sympathies and his advocacy of the romantic ethos show signs of collapse, for the fall of
Venice represents a perversion of that ethos, the historical moment at
which the noble, expressive spirit of the Gothic workman gives way to
the self-indulgent and haughty individualism of the Renaissance
artist. As I detail in the following chapters, Ruskin's comments on the
"romantic" in *The Lectures on Architecture and Painting, The Art of England*, and elsewhere demonstrate that he associates the romantic with
the Gothic. For Ruskin, the Renaissance represents the romantic
spirit of the Goth gone bad, rotted from within by the terrible afflictions of pride and infidelity. The result is the art of the "modern" post-medieval time, which typically reflects a perverted, dangerous notion
of individual freedom. Ruskin explicitly articulates this vision of
modern art as a fallen, corrupted romanticism in his series of Oxford
lectures, *Val D'Arno*, but it informs both his distinction between the
true and the false grotesque in *The Stones of Venice* and his famous formulation of the pathetic fallacy three years later in *Modern Painters III*.

In Pater's hands these discriminations are neutralized. He consistently recasts the older critic's prejudices as irrelevancies, particularly
Ruskin's theological bias and his distrust of modern poetry's animistic
efforts. The foundations of their aesthetic theories, however, are similar. Both Pater and Ruskin approach art as the expression of a unique
spirit and personality, and their theories reflect that tension between
the transcendental and the empirical that is an important legacy of romantic philosophy. For Ruskin, this opposition culminates in his conception of the pathetic fallacy, which stands as his failed attempt to
defend against the idolatrist tendency of the imagination, the danger
of mistaking an imaginative or fictive projection for a vision of the object's true nature. But Ruskin's formulation depends on his faith in a
truth that transcends rhetoric, thereby resulting in a moral distinction

between genuine and counterfeit imaginative perception. Pater utterly separates rhetoric from belief, echoing the Wordsworthian notion of "sincerity" in art as the accurate representation of the artist's feelings and vision. Ruskinian "sincerity," the imagination's noble confession "of its own ideality" (8:58), is obsolete in confrontation with Pater's dismissal of transcendent truths, for there is no truth of which to be deceived.[13]

By purging Ruskin's theory of its transcendental bias, Pater effectively counters Ruskin's critique of modern romanticism. In itself, Pater's rejection of the transcendental claims of Ruskin's idealism is not remarkable, for he is merely following the position maintained by contemporary empiricists, like Mill, whose influence at Oxford was substantial. But unlike most empiricist thinkers of his day, Pater demonstrates a deep sympathy for the idealist tradition, a sympathy all the more compelling because of his unwavering commitment to philosophical skepticism. In his transformation of Ruskin, Pater bequeaths to the moderns an ironic stance toward romantic transcendence and originality that simultaneously acknowledges the inescapable will to vision as well as the will to modernity, the desire to make it new. "He taught us to walk upon a rope, tightly stretched through serene air," only to be left suspended there "upon a swaying rope in a storm," Yeats complained (201). Romantic vision is for Pater both an ideal and an impossibility, and this largely accounts for the distinctive emotional tone of his writing. His late romantic obsessions with individual feeling and experience, the dangers of solipsism, and the sacerdotal function of the artist are informed by an empirical belief in the primacy of sensation and the relativity of knowledge.

Pater and Ruskin have been linked since their own day. For example, Oscar Wilde, in his first published essay, took the occasion to announce a modern-day English Renaissance, "that revival of culture and love of beauty which in great part owes its birth to Mr. Ruskin, and which Mr. Swinburne, and Mr. Pater, . . . and many others, are fostering and keeping alive, each in his own particular fashion" (quoted in Ellmann, *Oscar Wilde*, 81). But despite Wilde's precocious association of the two critics—indeed despite the scores of critics who have followed in Wilde's footsteps—the enigma of their relationship remains. In his translation of Ruskin's *The Bible of Amiens*, Marcel Proust notes that Pater's "Notre-Dame d'Amiens" is clearly indebted to Ruskin's conception of the cathedral, and remarks with puzzled disapproval, "I do not know why Ruskin's name is never once mentioned" (83). Indeed, Ruskin's name is never mentioned in any of Pater's published writing, with the exception of a brief footnote to his 1885 review of Ernest Chesneau's *The School of English Painting* identifying "a Preface by Professor Ruskin."[14] For that matter Pater rarely mentions any of his textual sources, and there are a great many of them. Critics generally agree that Pater's importance in nineteenth-century intellectual history depends less on the originality of his ideas than on his ability to assimilate and synthesize so many aspects of contemporary thought, including British empiricism, German idealism, contemporary science, and contemporary French and English literature. As Billie Andrew Inman explains, Pater is not alone among Victorian prose writers in compiling a large number of intellectual debts, but his silence regarding the process is unusual (*Pater's Reading*, xv).[15] Unlike Mill, Newman, Darwin, Carlyle, Arnold, and Ruskin, Pater neither kept a journal nor wrote an autobiography nor any other essay describing his major intellectual influences, and his letters reveal almost nothing.

Regarding Pater's intellectual relationship to Ruskin, therefore, we possess very little direct evidence—a brief reference to each other in the letters, and one reported incident. This material suggests something of a critical rivalry between the two, or at least on Pater's part. Benson reports that one of Pater's friends remembers talking about Ruskin when Pater uncharacteristically asserted, "I cannot believe that Ruskin saw more in the church of St. Mark than I do" (185). The only mention of Ruskin in Pater's letters betrays similar competitive ambitions. Responding to an inquiry by the journalist Henry James

Nicoll, Pater claims that he, not Ruskin, was the first English critic to discover Botticelli. "It [Pater's essay on Botticelli] preceded Mr. Ruskin's lectures on the same subject by I believe two years" (*Letters*, 41).[16] Ruskin, too, refers to Pater only once in his letters, remarking to his secretary that in looking over Pater's article on Botticelli he was surprised to find how much his thinking on the artist had changed, "for I recollect thinking Pater's article did him full justice—and now—though quite *right*—it reads lukewarm to me" (Claiborne, 307–8). According to Ruskin's early biographer, W. G. Collingwood, Ruskin quoted "with appreciation" Pater's description of Botticelli's Venus Anadyomene in his 1872 Oxford lectures, *Ariadne Florentina*, although the quotation does not appear in any published version of the lectures (Collingwood, 298). Eleven years later Ruskin had forgotten Pater's essay, or he had chosen to forget it. In the 1883 Epilogue to *Modern Painters* he claims that "it was left to me, and to me alone, first to discern, and then to teach . . . the excellency and supremacy of five great painters, despised until I spoke of them,—Turner, Tintoret, Luini, Botticelli, and Carpaccio" (4:355–56).[17]

In his 1949 book, *The Last Romantics*, Graham Hough first traced the roots of modernism to the romantic revival known as the English aesthetic movement and to its central figures: Ruskin, Pater, Rossetti, Morris, the Rhymers, and finally, Yeats. Twenty years later Hough's thesis was challenged by David DeLaura, who argued that "Pater seems distinctly out of place in this scheme" and claimed that "Hough does not establish the long-supposed link between Ruskin and Pater" (*Hebrew and Hellene*, ix). Following T. S. Eliot, DeLaura establishes the connection between Pater and his other most important contemporary influence, Matthew Arnold, tracing the development of aestheticism to Arnold's and Pater's transformation of religious doctrine as they found it in Newman's Christian humanism. But the long-supposed link between Pater and Ruskin, despite thirty more years of speculative criticism, is still not adequately established. That Pater embraced much of Ruskin's aesthetic theory while purging it of its

moral and theological bias is today something of a critical commonplace, but the lack of any detailed study obscures and simplifies this
important line of inheritance in Victorian culture.

The most provocative analysis we have of the Pater-Ruskin relationship remains Harold Bloom's 1974 essay, "The Crystal Man."
"Pater's context," Bloom claims, "begins with his only begetter, Ruskin,
whose effect can be read, frequently through negation, throughout
Pater's work" (x).[18] While most readers do not recognize a Pater of
such uncomplicated lineage, critics of the last twenty-five years have
generally followed Bloom by suggesting that Pater "implicitly sub-
verts," "tacitly revises," "reverses," "transforms," "reweaves," "reworks,"
"absorbs," "crystallizes," even "kills off" the massive intellectual and psychological presence of Ruskin. Perhaps the most sustained critical attention has focused on Pater's and Ruskin's relationship within the
nineteenth-century "literature of art" tradition. Richard Stein traces
Pater's debt to Ruskin as a practitioner of this Victorian prose genre
while outlining his efforts, in both *The Renaissance* and his imaginary
portraits, to develop a historical method and "moral aesthetic" distinct
from Ruskin.[19] Pater's treatment of the Italian Renaissance is his most
conspicuous reversal of Ruskin, but while it is often alluded to, only a
handful of critics besides Stein have addressed the subject beyond isolated observations and general reflections (Bullen, "Pater and Ruskin"
and *Myth of the Renaissance*, 273–98; Harris, "Ruskin and Pater"; Fraser,
212–56).[20]

In another direction, Joseph Bizup and James Eli Adams have recently suggested that Ruskin's account of the "gentleman" as a man distinguished by an innate capacity to experience sensation provides
Pater with a model of masculinity he manipulates to assert the morality of his aestheticism and to authorize the "centrality of the male
body" in his construction of the Hellenic tradition (Adams, 149–81).[21]
Robert and Janice A. Keefe have laid the foundations for a study of
Ruskin's presence in Pater's thinking on Greek art and mythology,
emphasizing the impact on Pater of "Ruskin's idea of chiaroscuro in

Greek art" (52–83).[22] Finally, Jonathan Loesberg's brief but compelling discussion neatly summarizes the method of Pater's revisionary response to Ruskin by suggesting that Pater's more "inclusive" aestheticism encompasses both Ruskin's aesthetic theory and his evaluation of history (34–41, 54–60).[23]

Pater's revisionary response to Ruskin does not usually take the form of direct confrontation. Although he addresses the same subjects as Ruskin and appropriates many of Ruskin's critical positions, Pater decisively shifts the ground of discussion. His philosophical and linguistic premises are radically distinct from Ruskin's even when he invokes the older critic's presence in references and allusions.

As scholars have long recognized, Pater's writing is highly allusive. The art historian Elizabeth Prettejohn suggests that Pater's many references are part of a "vast intertextual network" that links his writing to other works of the aesthetic movement. The prevalence in aestheticist art of shared references to specific motifs, she argues, creates "a distinctive form of group identity" (47). But, as Prettejohn notes, the range of reference in Pater is complex and diverse, complicating the formation of aestheticism's group identity and the relation of that group to a larger public audience. While many of Pater's allusions are openly asserted, others are deliberately covert and unacknowledged, thereby obscuring any intertextual link. Still others claim derivation from a nonexistent text, or from a text that does not contain the words Pater attributes to it. This is the Pater who provokes the ire of T. S. Eliot and Christopher Ricks, both of whom regard his habit of bogus allusion and misquotation—what Ricks calls his "re-creative mistranscriptions" (405)—as the vampiric appropriation of another, more genuine creation. "Pater demeans his authors by outdoing them," Ricks writes, "escalating their phrases into his fugitive noosphere" (408).

In her account of Pater's frequent allusions to Baudelaire, Patricia Clements analyzes the Paterian type of covert allusion. While Pater refers to Baudelaire by name only twice in his career—the 1876 "Ro-

manticism" and the 1890 lecture on Mérimée—Clements argues that
the French poet is "the master of much of [Pater's] critical thought,"

> but he took the greatest care to ensure that his acknowledgment
> would be apparent only to very few of his readers. . . . In [Pater],
> allusion and the manipulation of what is often literally a sub-
> text are masterful: they are carefully and consciously cultivated
> defenses and delicately controlled instruments of meaning. (80)

According to Clements, the systematic suppression of the name
Baudelaire is a typical manifestation of Pater's style, with its emphasis
on restraint and its frequent layering of multiple subtexts. But in the
particular case of Baudelaire, Clements describes Pater as being more
than usually careful and covert. His allusions to the dangerous French
poet, dubbed by Robert Buchanan the "godfather . . . of the modern
Fleshly School" (21), were meant to be detected by only a select inner
circle of readers for whom he could safely express his debt and admiration. David Carrier reads the evidence of Clements's study differ-
ently. Rather than the provocative intimation of a secret alliance,
Carrier reads Pater's allusions to Baudelaire as an aggressive critique
of the poet's conception of modern art. In effect, Pater uses Baudelaire
to distinguish his own theory of modernity. "Taking Baudelaire's conception of modernist beauty," Carrier argues, "he transforms it" (119).

In the following pages, I describe how Pater self-consciously uses
and transforms Ruskin to distinguish his own moral, aesthetic, and
sociopolitical values. Pater's allusiveness, along with other stylistic tendencies toward disjunction, postponement, and qualification, helps to
account for his extreme elusiveness. He is not easy to pin down. As
Denis Donoghue observes, "Pater rarely speaks for himself; normally
he lets his feelings emerge from his attention to something else"
(308)—and in the voice of somebody else, we might add. "Quotation,"
as Carrier reminds us, "involves a kind of ventriloquism, an author
speaking with a borrowed voice" (110). Pater's unacknowledged

quotations (and misquotations) tend to obscure those borrowed voices. Depending on his reader, Pater's text is more or less allusive. But whether we recognize the allusions or not, they work to declare allegiances, suggest alliances, make alterations and appropriations. In recent years, intertextuality has supplanted influence as a means of conceptualizing literary history (Clayton and Rothstein). But like influence, intertextuality has a great many different theories, ranging from Roland Barthes's emphasis on the infinite renewal of interpretation to Michael Riffaterre's efforts to achieve interpretive certainty. Most theories of intertextuality, however, are consistent in their effort to read texts without positing a free and autonomous author.

In contrast, much practical literary criticism, especially in America, does not require the "death of the author" as a precondition of intertextual readings.[24] In his recent *Byron and the Victorians*, Andrew Elfenbein concludes that "[r]ather than fundamentally challenging the literary work's status, intertextuality has merely provided an attitude toward textual origins, a reminder that they are never self-generating" (2). He historicizes Byron's influence on the Victorians, thereby emphasizing "the role of institutions and reception as catalysts" for subjective agency (4). In another recent study, Antony Harrison preserves the subjective agency of the author while scrutinizing the "self-consciously intertextual uses of precursors by Victorian poets," revealing the sociopolitical, moral, and aesthetic values reflected in each poet's work (1). "Intertextuality," argues Harrison, "can only artificially and arbitrarily extricate itself from the historically particular situations of the systems that are its objects of analysis" (9). Something like this historicized view is much closer to my approach.

In describing how Pater manages to create a fruitful relationship with Ruskin's texts, I obviously insist on a degree of authorial agency in the construction of that relationship. Indeed, I will be at pains to demonstrate how well Pater understands precisely what is at stake in his dialogue with Ruskin on romanticism. But at the same time I have attempted to relate the reading and writing activities of Pater and Ruskin to specific historical constraints and opportunities. For instance, my analysis of each writer's reception of Wordsworth is related to the larger Victorian construction and diffusion of Wordsworth. The crucial place *The Excursion* holds in the poet's oeuvre, the relatively unimportant place held by *The Prelude* after its publication in 1850, the widespread perception of Wordsworth's poetry as an anodyne for the hardships of modern life—these and other examples of the Victorian sense of what constitutes Wordsworth fashion Ruskin's and Pater's reading of the poet. Similarly, what constitutes their Italian Renaissance derives from the scholarly discoveries of nineteenth-century Renaissance historiography. While at Oxford, both critics worked within a professional hierarchy that clearly favored Ruskin. I therefore read Pater's essays, particularly those written during Ruskin's time at Oxford, as efforts to establish institutional prestige and recognition as a critic of the fine arts. At the same time, I analyze the constraints faced by Ruskin as a lecturer in the Oxford system. Throughout the study, I demonstrate that Pater carefully argued against Ruskin's theory of romanticism and the Tory authoritarianism that undergirded it, mounting his own theory of romanticism to which modern criticism is substantially indebted.

My first chapter details Pater's response to Ruskin's critique of nineteenth-century English poetry by tracing each critic's reception of Wordsworth. Pater conceives of Wordsworth's poetry as embodying a historically recurrent form of animism, thereby revising Ruskin's history of landscape art and overturning his notion of the pathetic fallacy as the fallen remnant of an earlier authentic belief in myth. Chapter 2 extends both critics' readings of Wordsworth to their respective visions of the Italian Renaissance. Focusing especially on the 1867 essay "Winckelmann," I argue that Pater's history of artistic ideals both critiques the historical narrative of Ruskin's *The Stones of Venice* and endorses Ruskin's own revision of that narrative.

The first part of the book establishes the foundations of each critic's theory of romanticism. I turn in the second part to the years in which both Pater and Ruskin taught at Oxford, emphasizing the immediate context of the Oxford literary culture of the 1870s. More than one critic has speculated that Ruskin's presence in Oxford as Slade Professor of Fine Art provoked Pater to a direct challenge (Fishman, 48–49; Bullen, "Pater and Ruskin"; Leng). Building on these observations, I argue that Pater's essays on Michelangelo and Romanticism revise, almost point for point, Ruskin's Oxford lectures on the same topics. Chapter 3 considers the correspondence between Pater's essays and Ruskin's lectures on Michelangelo. The chapter includes an analysis of both critics' reception of Leonardo da Vinci, illustrating their competing theories of the Italian Renaissance as an expression of the romantic spirit. The last chapter analyzes each critic's fullest theoretical articulation of the term "romanticism"—Ruskin's 1873 Oxford lecture "Franchise" and Pater's 1876 essay "Romanticism." I conclude by tracing continuities between the Pater-Ruskin opposition and subsequent Anglo-American disagreements over the nature of romanticism.

In the course of establishing the textual evidence I address a range of issues confronting Victorian intellectuals, including liberalism, historiography, and anthropology. But my chief aim is to demonstrate that Ruskin's attitude toward the modern romantic revival inspires Pater's defense of that revival, culminating in his rescue of romanticism.

One 🔖 The Wordsworth of Pater and Ruskin

R USKIN'S critical reception of Wordsworth typifies his ambivalent response to modern romantic art. While Walter Scott stands as the modern English poet who comes closest to Ruskin's romantic ideal, Wordsworth exemplifies the characteristic failings, as well as the glories, of the nineteenth-century revival of romance. For Pater, the English poets Morris and Rossetti and Coleridge and even Byron are more quintessentially "romantic" than Wordsworth, and French literature produces the "most characteristic expression" of the romantic temper ("Romanticism," 67).[1] But it is in the essay on Wordsworth that Pater most fully elaborates a crucial element in his conception of romantic art—the transformation of the material world through the power of individual temperament, what Ruskin calls the pathetic fallacy. The "perfect fidelity to one's own inward presentations" is the requisite act of Pater's romantic artist resulting in that certain distortion or strangeness that is the requisite condition of romantic art ("On Wordsworth," 459). Despite his tranquillity and sense of well-being, personality traits Pater does not associate with the romantic spirit, Pater's Wordsworth is a romantic author of strange and beautiful objects. He is a poet of a "certain difficult way" whose readers, "like people who have passed through some initiation" (456), recognize his power to "dissolve" the "actual world" and lift them "to a world altogether different in its vagueness and vastness" (462).[2] Pater's reading transforms Ruskin's ambivalence regarding Wordsworth into the essence of his own theory of the romantic.

Ruskin's Evangelical Wordsworth

From the *Lectures on Architecture and Painting* (1854) through the Oxford lectures, *The Art of England* (1883), Ruskin uses the word "romantic," as he says, "always in a noble sense" (33:269). Romantic feeling is "instinctive" and "true" and is opposed to all that is vulgar, stupid, and dishonorable. Ruskin variously characterizes the romantic as heroic, passionate, imaginative, virtuous, beautiful, modest, sincere, and sublime. "A man's conscience," he asserts, "may be utterly perverted and led astray but so long as the feelings of romance endure within us, they are unerring,—they are as true to what is right and lovely as the needle to the north" (12:55). The emphasis on "unerring" highlights Ruskin's idealized vision of romance, suppressing the concept of erring that is an essential component of medieval romance. For Ruskin, romance is simply the sum of all "the holiest principles of humanity" (12:55). But as such it is nostalgic, even reactionary, for it is expressive of an ethical temper and political fabric he believes has generally disappeared, one he most specifically identifies with the Christian art of the Middle Ages: "the great evil of these days is that we try to destroy the romantic feeling, instead of bridling and directing it" (12:55).[3] His reception of modern romantic art, then, is seemingly inconsistent in that it reflects a tension between his joyful discernment of a romantic revival in nineteenth-century poetry and painting and his disgust at what he perceives as the modern perversion of romance, the transformation of "loyalty into license, protection into plunder, truth into treachery, chivalry into selfishness" (12:56).

Ruskin's lifelong preoccupation with Wordsworth reflects that tension. In 1880, near the end of his career, Ruskin could write that he had "used Wordsworth as a daily text-book from youth to age, and ha[d] lived, moreover, in all essential points according to the tenor of his teaching" (34:349). But in the very same series of essays, later published as *Fiction, Fair and Foul,* the tenor of the poet's teaching is the subject of Ruskin's most scathing sarcasm: "I much doubt there being many inglorious Miltons in our country churchyard; but I am very sure there are many Wordsworths resting there, who were inferior to the renowned one only in caring less to hear themselves talk" (34:319). Throughout *Fiction, Fair and Foul* and other late writings Ruskin's comments on Wordsworth are largely unkind, alternating between affectionate condescension and outright condemnation. His greatest objection is to the poet's arrogance, the noisy tenor of his way. "Who thinks of self, when gazing on the sky?" asks Ruskin, quoting a line from Byron's poem, *The Island* (1823). "Well, I don't know; Mr. Wordsworth certainly did, and observed, with truth, that its clouds took a sober coloring in consequence of his experiences" (34:325). Wordsworth runs throughout the book as a foil to Byron and Burns and Scott, the three "strange prophets" of modern life. Ruskin clearly wants to raise Byron above Wordsworth in his estimation of the two poets' value to the modern reader, opposing not only Arnold but also Hazlitt and Mill, who each compared Wordsworth favorably to Byron.

As his career progressed, Ruskin's critical response to Wordsworth grew increasingly antagonistic. But until the publication of *Modern Painters III* in 1856 he betrays no misgivings about the poet's value to the modern reader. "Wordsworth," he writes in a letter to his tutor at Christ Church, "may be trusted as a guide in everything, he feels nothing but what we ought all to feel—what every mind in pure moral health *must* feel, he says nothing but what we all ought to believe—what all strong intellects *must* believe" (4:392). In *Modern Painters I,* from 1843, Wordsworth is continuously invoked in defense of Turner's depictions of nature, of sky and sunlight and clouds and mountain vapors: "hear how Wordsworth, the keenest-eyed of all modern poets for what is deep and essential in nature, illustrates

Turner here, as we shall find him doing in all other points" (3:307; quoted in Bate, 67–68). The illustrations Ruskin takes from Wordsworth are primarily from the long descriptive-meditative poem *The Excursion,* Ruskin's favorite poem of Wordsworth's and the poem he believed could best teach the ordinary nineteenth-century spectator how to see. As Elizabeth Helsinger explains, *The Excursion* provided Ruskin with a model of "excursive sight," that manner of seeing associated with the traveler's leisurely progress through landscape and distinguished from the sublime sight of the poet or artist, those intense, imaginatively transformed encounters with nature recorded in Wordsworth's "Poems of the Imagination." *The Excursion* represents "the education of wandering spectators by a wandering sage," and as such it served as a model for Ruskin's "efforts to encourage and reform" the everyday person's habits of perception (Helsinger, 93).[4] As a moral guide for the apprehension of the natural world, Wordsworth's Wanderer stresses not only visual perception but also the human and social relevance of the encounter, providing various historical, personal, and social perspectives from which to view nature. This is the Wordsworth that provided Ruskin the foundation of, in the words of Jonathan Bate, "a programme for education into ecological consciousness" (84).

This same Wordsworth, for Ruskin and many other Victorian readers, also created the greatest work of Christian art in the nineteenth century (Gill, 63–70; Prickett).[5] As the embodiment of the Christian values of selflessness, faith, and charity, the Wanderer, a pedlar of Calvinist disposition, reflects the religious vision that informs all of Ruskin's own work. Ruskin proclaimed *The Excursion* the "crown" of Wordsworth's poetry (4:393), a "thoroughly religious book" (*Ruskin's Letters,* 92).[6] His favorite part of the poem was Book IV, "Despondency Corrected," in which the Wanderer, in an effort to relieve the Solitary's sorrow and cynicism, asserts the healing power of belief in a benevolent superintending providence. "We live by admiration, hope, and love" (IV, 763), the Wanderer counsels, approximating St.

Paul's enunciation of the three Evangelical virtues.[7] It is one of
Ruskin's favorite lines in all of Wordsworth, and he turned to it
repeatedly—to describe the apprehension of beauty (4:29), to clarify
the goals of Political Economy (27:90), to define "poetical feeling"
(5:28). In notes written toward the end of his career Ruskin claimed
that this "one line of Wordsworth's" represents "the teaching and main
dividing of all that I have . . . written."

> Understanding always that the admiration is not of ourselves
> only, and the hope not for ourselves only. I do not add, the love
> not of ourselves only, for, often as we use the word, self-love is a
> contradiction in terms. Love *can* be only of others; only vulgar
> pride, vulgar indulgence, can centre in ourselves. (22:505)

Ruskin's dismissal of self-love is explicitly endorsed by the Wanderer
later in Book IV in the well-known lines that Ruskin used as the epigraph to *Modern Painters*.

Accuse me not
Of arrogance . . .
If, having walked with Nature,
And offered, far as frailty would allow,
My heart a daily sacrifice to Truth,
I now affirm of Nature and of Truth,
Whom I have served, that their Divinity
Revolts, offended at the ways of men,
Philosophers, who, though the human soul
Be of a thousand faculties composed,
And twice ten thousand interests, do yet prize
This soul, and the transcendent universe,
No more than as a mirror that reflects
To proud Self-love her own intelligence.
(IV, 978–92)

The Wanderer's righteous assertion against egotism and vanity greets readers as they open each volume of *Modern Painters*, associating the moral vision of the Anglican poet laureate with that of the younger critic of contemporary art.

But even within the pages of *Modern Painters*, Ruskin portrays a Wordsworth who too often falls short of the moral standard set by his Wanderer. Indeed, after the publication of *Modern Painters III* it must have struck some readers that the book's epigraph was an invocation of Wordsworth against Wordsworth, for in that volume Ruskin declares the poet guilty of self-love, the very offense against which Divinity and the critic revolt. Subsequent readers have suggested that *The Excursion* itself is a kind of reflexive response by Wordsworth against Wordsworth in that it calls into question the value of the poet's preoccupation with the growth of his own mind (Hickey; Galperin; Wolfson). The Wanderer's invective against self-love follows a passage that explicitly raises the whole question of *The Prelude* (Wolfson, 181).

> And if indeed there be
> An all-pervading Spirit, upon whom
> Our dark foundations rest, could he design
> That this magnificent effect of power,
> The earth we tread, the sky that we behold
> By day, and all the pomp which night reveals;
> That these—and that superior mystery
> Our vital frame, so fearfully devised,
> And the dread soul within it—should exist
> Only to be examined, pondered, searched,
> Probed, vexed, and criticized?
>
> (IV, 968–78)

Ruskin had most probably read *The Prelude* before the publication of *Modern Painters III*, although never once in all of the Library Edition does he mention or even allude to the poem. But his silence is telling, for it suggests a purposeful evasion of the work that most fully represents the Wordsworth to which he objects and which he believes is detrimental to the cultural health of contemporary England. In the third volume of *Modern Painters*, Ruskin for the first time expresses that objection. Wordsworth is representative of the modern tendency toward the pathetic fallacy, the self-indulgent perception of the natural world that obscures the apprehension of nature as a gift from God.[8] Lacking in self-restraint, he is too often fixated on his own feelings at the expense of the world around him. Ruskin describes Wordsworth as deficient in humility, affected in his simplicity, and indifferent toward the structural dynamics of the natural world.

In his book on Ruskin's religious faith, *Nature's Covenant,* Stephen Finley suggests that such poems as *The Excursion,* "The White Doe of Rylstone," and the *Ecclesiastical Sonnets,* "permeated as they are by the language of orthodox Christian theology, established the tenor of Wordsworth's poetry as a whole for Ruskin" (123), and he argues that "Ruskin knew no other poet than this 'thoroughly religious' Wordsworth" (124). Finley is skeptical about the influential formulation of Victorian antiromanticism or anti-Wordsworthianism, especially with regard to Ruskin, and he is right to distinguish "the modern Wordsworth whose centrality to romanticism is defined by *The Prelude*" from Ruskin's Wordsworth whose "career is defined by its relation to *The Excursion*" (120). But the Wordsworth of "the self-reflecting consciousness" is not unknown to Ruskin.[9] That poet comes into view when we turn away from *The Excursion* and look at Ruskin's reception of Wordsworth's "Poems of the Imagination," especially the "Intimations" ode. Next to *The Excursion,* Ruskin quotes from the ode more than from any other of Wordsworth's poems. He evokes the poem for a variety of reasons, using it as both an adversarial and a supportive text in his arguments, or simply as a starting point for his reflections on custom, memory, death, the beauty of nature, the spiritual life of children, and the role of the imagination in response to the natural world. Taken together, Ruskin's lifelong response to the ode neatly illustrates the ambivalence he feels toward Wordsworth and especially toward the poet's role in both the modern revival and the perversion of romance.

Ruskin's Egotistical Wordsworth

Loss and consolation are subjects that haunt the Victorian imagination, and many Victorian poems and novels explicitly evoke
Wordsworth's "Intimations" ode. As Antony Harrison observes, the
ode's mythos "constitutes a thematic foundation and a body of transcendental assumptions in Victorian literary texts" (170).[10] Lawrence
Kramer characterizes the ode as "the central and indispensable articulation of the Romantic dialectic in which the self seeks imaginative
compensation for the loss of its capacity to experience the world as a
radiant plenitude" and then argues that Victorian writers seem com-
pelled to define their search for compensation "against the pattern established by the 'Intimations' Ode" (316). The ode is one of the most
influential nineteenth-century revivals of the redemptive pattern of
romance. That Wordsworthian pattern, however, undergoes a radical
change at the hands of Victorian writers who are less willing to regard
the individual powers of memory and imagination as adequate rec-
ompense for the loss of an earlier self. In the words of Carol T. Christ:

> The Victorians could not feel this compensatory exaltation.
> The fear implicit in Romanticism that we may fail to know the
> objects of our consciousness, that we may realize only an eccen-
> tric and personal reality, motivates Victorian attempts to turn
> from what they perceive as a disabling focus upon the self. (5)

Victorian writers are endlessly innovative in their skeptical responses
to the Wordsworthian faith in memory and imagination as sources of
renovation. They assail the isolated imagination as narcissistic and destructive, or, more modestly, as an impediment to human relation-
ships, holding up love as a more natural and affirming source of
compensation. They expose memory and imagination as demonic and
frightening forces, or debunk the myth of renovation, revealing it to be
delusional and dangerous, a naive act of wish fulfillment.

In Tennyson's "Oenone," for example, the forsaken nymph frantically seeks some degree of consolation for the loss of Paris and her earlier self. Oenone ultimately turns inward and achieves a kind of apocalyptic solipsism:

> What this may be I know not, but I know
> That, wheresoe'er I am by night and day,
> All earth and air seem only burning fire.
>
> (262–64)[11]

In these closing lines of "Oenone," Tennyson uses the phrase from Wordsworth's ode in its opposite context. Whereas in Wordsworth "Turn wheresoe'er I may, / By night or day" occurs at the beginning of the poem in which a glory has passed away from the earth, Tennyson uses the phrase to mark the achievement of Oenone's vision. Furthermore, and more importantly in my context, Oenone's vision is found wanting—"All earth and air seem *only* burning fire" (my italics), emphasizing not the glory and intensity of perpetual fire, but instead what is absent from that condition, namely, Paris (Tucker, 172–74).

In "Dover Beach," Matthew Arnold methodically undercuts the visual imagery from Wordsworth's ode—the earth appareled in celestial light, waters on a starry night, children sporting on the shore—and represents Wordsworth's faith in the "seeing" powers of memory and imagination as illusory and deceptive (Timko, 59). In his 1879 selection of Wordsworth's poetry, Arnold placed the "Intimations" ode in a section entitled "Poems Akin to the Antique, and Odes," defying Wordsworth's express desire that the ode stand alone in any edition of his poems (Knoepflmacher, "Mutations," 400). In his "Preface" to that selection Arnold critiques Wordsworth's "philosophic system" by questioning the logic and authenticity of the ode's pattern of experience.

> Even the "intimations of" of the famous Ode, those cornerstones of the supposed philosophic system of Wordsworth,—the idea of the high instincts and affections coming out in

childhood, testifying of a divine home recently left, and fading away as our life proceeds,—this idea, of undeniable beauty as a play of fancy, has itself not the character of poetic truth of the best kind; it has no real solidity. . . . [T]o say that universally this instinct is mighty in childhood, and tends to die afterwards, is to say what is extremely doubtful. In many people, perhaps with the majority of educated persons, the love of nature is nearly imperceptible at ten years old, but strong and operative at thirty. (9:49–50)[12]

Arnold's comment is a pragmatic interrogation of Wordsworth's idealized child of nature.

Swinburne conveyed a more agitated and hostile response to the myth of immortality inaugurated in the "Intimations" ode. Writing about Arnold's poetry in his 1867 essay, "Matthew Arnold's New Poems," Swinburne deplores Wordsworth's "inveterate and invincible Philistinism," which he finds most powerfully, and therefore most dangerously, expressed in the ode. The ode's myth of immortality is the "unwholesome" result of "Wordsworth's spirit of compromise with the nature of things" (Complete Works, 15:86–87). As Antony Harrison points out, Swinburne often figures death "using Wordsworth's central metaphor of immortality, the sea" (180).[13]

Like his contemporaries, Ruskin is obsessed with the language and images of the ode. Unlike Arnold, Ruskin wholly internalized the pattern of experience described by the poem, so his rejection of Wordsworth's myth of renovation is especially powerful. Cook and Wedderburn comment that as early as the composition of Modern Painters II Ruskin was "conscious at times of losing something of his earliest rapture" (4:77). Diary entries and letters from these years, his mid-twenties, persistently express a loss of childhood enthusiasm and feeling for nature. In a letter to Walter Brown, his old tutor at Christ Church, Ruskin describes his experience, as Harold Bloom recognizes, in "phrases directly borrowed from the 'Intimations' Ode" ("Introduction," xix):

there was a time when the sight of a steep hill covered with pines cutting against blue sky, would have touched me with an emotion inexpressible, which, in the endeavour to communicate in its truth and intensity, I must have sought for all kinds of far-off, wild, and dreamy images. Now I can look at such a slope with coolness, and observation of *fact*. I see that it slopes at twenty or twenty-five degrees; I know the pines are spruce fir— "Pinus nigra"—of such and such a formation; the soil, thus, and thus; the day fine and the sky blue. All this I can at once communicate in so many words, and this is all which is necessarily seen. But it is not all the truth: there is something else to be seen there, which I cannot see but in a certain condition of mind, nor can I make anyone else see it, but by putting him into that condition, and my endeavour in description would be, not to detail the facts of the scene, but by any means whatsoever to put my hearer's mind into the same ferment as my mind. (36:80)

Throughout his career, Ruskin remained sympathetic to the ode's depiction of the child's high instincts and perceptive powers, and of the inevitable fading of those powers.

Not surprisingly, then, when Ruskin sets out in *Modern Painters II* to distinguish "qualities or types" (4:76) of beauty he asks his reader to approach the subject, "as far as may be, as a little child, ridding himself of all conventional and authoritative thoughts" (4:77).[14] The perception of beauty, Ruskin insists, depends upon a simplicity of feeling in the perceiver, and he turns to Wordsworth's ode to describe these early perceptions when we have freshly awakened to the sense of the beautiful:

I suppose there are few among those who love Nature otherwise than by profession and at second-hand, who look not back to their youngest and least-learned days as those of the most intense, superstitious, insatiable, and beatific perception of her splendours. And the bitter decline of this glorious feeling though many note it not, partly owing to the cares and weight of manhood, which leave them not the time nor the liberty to look for their lost treasure, and partly to the human and divine affections which are appointed to take its place, yet has formed the subject, not indeed of lamentation, but of holy thankfulness for the witness it bears to the immortal origin and end of our nature, to one whose authority is almost without appeal in all questions relating to the influence of external things upon the pure human soul. (4:77–78)

Ruskin then quotes the passage from the poem beginning "Heaven lies about us in our infancy." He fervently endorses the subject of the ode in which the bitter decline of the child's perceptive powers is cause not for "lamentation" but for "holy thankfulness." And he seemingly accepts the notion that other "human and divine affections . . . are appointed" to take [the] place of "beatific" perceptions.

By 1883, however, when he published a new edition of *Modern Painters II*, Ruskin could not let the passage stand without comment. Regarding the ode's central claim that the glories of childhood bear "witness . . . to the immortal origin and end of our nature," Ruskin now replies:

> To the origin and *purpose* of it, yes; but not to the immortality of it,—else the lamb might be proved as immortal as its slaughterer. Wordsworth is indeed "almost without appeal" as to the impressions of natural things on the human mind,—but by no means as to the logical conclusions to be surely drawn from them. (4:78)

The 1883 edition of the second volume of *Modern Painters* provides enormous insight into the changes of Ruskin's thought from his early to later years, and Ruskin's note nicely indicates the shift in his attitude toward the poet. Despite Wordsworth's vivid sense of natural beauty, he could not be trusted as a moral philosopher. Ruskin had come to regard Wordsworth's philosophical speculations as too facile and self-absorbed. As he writes in *Praeterita*, "On the journey of 1837, when I was eighteen, I felt, for the last time, the pure childish love of nature which Wordsworth so idly takes for an intimation of immortality" (35:218). The "holy thankfulness" that in 1846 Ruskin believes characterizes the sentiment expressed in Wordsworth's ode has turned to illogic and idleness in the mid-1880s.

In *Fiction, Fair and Foul* Ruskin represents Wordsworth as an unfit role model for contemporary England. As compared to Scott or Burns or Byron, Wordsworth is deficient in social conscience and social action. Though "sweet and precious," he is obsolete and inadequate, capable of providing only temporary relief from the "fever of the restless and corrupted life around him" (34:318). Ruskin turns to the language and imagery of the ode to emphasize the poet's limitations.

> A measured mind, and calm; innocent, unrepentant; helpful to sinless creatures and scatheless, such of the flock as do not stray. Hopeful at least, if not faithful; content with intimations of immortality such as may be in skipping of lambs and laughter of children—incurious to see in the hands the print of the Nails. (34:320)

In Ruskin's later reading, the ode provides its readers a justification for ignoring the realities of life "inland," focusing their gaze instead on the prelapsarian shores of that immortal sea. The ills and immediacies of concrete experience are obscured by the preoccupations of consciousness and memory. Thinking of himself while gazing on the sky, Wordsworth observes that the clouds take on a sober coloring. Ruskin's England was in need of a very different moral education.

Even Ruskin's praise of the poet is highly qualified. He admires Wordsworth's portrait of a "wholesome" country life, but his admiration is mingled with condescension.

With an honest and kindly heart, a stimulating egoism, a
wholesome contentment in modest circumstances, and such
sufficient ease, in that accepted state, as permitted the passing of
a good deal of time in wishing that daisies could see the beauty
of their own shadows, and other such profitable mental exer-
cises, Wordsworth has left us a series of studies of the graceful
and happy shepherd life of our lake country, which to me per-
sonally, for one, are entirely sweet and precious; but they are
only so as the mirror of an existent reality in many ways more
beautiful than its picture. (34:320)

In effect, Ruskin is paraphrasing the epigraph to *Modern Painters* taken
from *The Excursion* and transforming Wordsworth himself into one of
those self-indulgent philosophers. Wordsworth's picture of country
life is darkened, in Ruskin's view, by hubris and self-indulgence. The
virtuous feelings of the Cumberland peasantry are obscured by the
poet's ambition to be "the leader of a new and only correct school of
poetry" (34:320), and his "aerial" song never reaches "etherial" heights
but is instead made more "lowly in its privacy of light" (34:320).

Wordsworthian pastoral, according to Ruskin, is consequently
marred by the poet's insincerity. The "passion" of Burns, and Scott, and
Byron is "more true." For instance, Ruskin reads Wordsworth's description of the river Wharf's "mournful voice" as inconsistent with an
earlier passage of the poem and so proof of the poet's artificial feeling.
Or he chides Wordsworth for suggesting that "divine" thoughts arise
from leisurely meditation in a pastoral setting, arguing instead that an
upright posture may be a more fit "moral position" for divine reflections. As the last comment suggests, the aspersions of *Fiction, Fair and
Foul* sometimes reveal Ruskin at his most annoying, and most prig-
gish, as a literary critic.

Pater's Strange Wordsworth

The characters of Pater's historical and imaginary portraits are
each romantic heroes, which is to say that each pursues a Words-

worthian return to a "prior state of existence" (Wordsworth *The Poems*, 2:979).[15] Marius, Florian, Duke Carl of Rosenmold, Winckelmann, Leonardo, Plato, Coleridge, Rossetti, Wordsworth—each seeks to recover that instinctual, nondiscursive, immaterial relation to experience that Wordsworth located in childhood, and each confronts the existential danger associated with that quest. The narrator of Pater's "Denys L'Auxerrois" begins his deliberate telling of such a return with a well-advised warning:

> Almost every people, as we know, has had its legend of a "golden age" and of its return—legends which will hardly be forgotten, however prosaic the world may become, while man himself remains the aspiring, never quite contented being he is. And yet in truth, since we are no longer children, we might well question the advantage of a return to us of a condition of life in which, by the nature of the case, the values of things would, so to speak, lie wholly on their surfaces, unless we could regain also the childish consciousness, or rather unconsciousness, in ourselves, to take all that adroitly and with the appropriate lightness of heart. (*Imaginary Portraits*, 47)

We might well question the advantage of such a return because, as Denys/Dionysus reveals, it is likely to be accompanied by madness. The self-conscious apprehension of loss threatens the project of return from the beginning. Denys is one of Pater's darkest expressions of the "anxieties of self-consciousness," which are by the second half of the nineteenth century "a traditional part of [Pater's] late romantic literary culture" (Williams, 21).[16] The return to "childish consciousness" is shadowed by its familiar, a "dark or antipathetic side" (66), the savage, carnivorous Denys, bloody vine-axe in hand.

Pater's recognition of this antipathetic side informs his portrait of Wordsworth. He depicts a far darker and far stranger poet than that presented by most of his contemporaries. Victorian critics typically prescribed Wordsworth as a remedy for pain and suffering. John Stuart Mill most famously turned to the poet as a cure for depression, but a host of other Victorian essayists, among them William Knight, Leslie Stephens, and Matthew Arnold, emphasized the healing power of Wordsworth's poetry (Bourke; Perkins, 85–120; Logan). "What Wordsworth does," writes John Morley in the introduction to his 1888 edition of Wordsworth's poems, "is to assuage, to reconcile, to fortify" (lxiv). Pater's Wordsworth also maintains this fortifying function, serving as a kind of anodyne for the hardships of modern life. His poetry helps "to withdraw the thoughts for a little while from the mere machinery of life" and to fix them on the "great facts in man's existence." Possessing a "sort of religious placidity" (Pater, "On Wordsworth," 457), Wordsworth conveys to his readers "an extraordinary wisdom in the things of practice" (463). But the poet's wisdom is not easy and it is not immediately apparent. The "more powerful and original poet" is "hidden away" (465), buried under "received ideas" and conventional "religious sentiment" (461). Pater discovers the "secret attraction" of the poetry in its "sudden passage from lowly thoughts and places to the majestic forms of philosophical imagination" (462). In contrast to Arnold (and the later Ruskin), who complained that Wordsworth's poetry was deficient in thought, Pater argues that the poet courageously follows "bold trains of speculative thought" (461).

"Strange" and "peculiar" are the words repeated most often in Pater's essay. In his higher, more imaginative moments, Wordsworth skirts "the borders of this world" ("On Wordsworth," 462), deriving exceptional poetic power from his "strange contact" with traditions of mystical and philosophical speculation. Pater describes the poet, while absorbed in such periods of "intense susceptibility," as bordering on an extreme solipsism.

> Sometimes as he dwelt upon those moments of profound, imaginative power, in which the outward object appears to take colour and expression, a new nature almost, from the prompting of the observant mind, the actual world seemed to dissolve and detach itself, flake by flake, and he himself seemed to be the creator, and when he would the destroyer, of the world in which

he lived—that old isolating thought of many a brain-sick mystic of ancient and modern times. (461–62)

Surprisingly, many contemporary critics still fail to recognize that Pater inaugurated that tradition in Wordsworth criticism, first described by M. H. Abrams, that regards the poet as "problematic," a "complex poet of strangeness, paradox, equivocality, and dark sublimities" (Abrams, 2). Abrams himself overlooks Pater, identifying instead A. C. Bradley's 1909 essay as the *Ur*-text of the "problematic" Wordsworth. More recently, William Galperin aligns both Pater and Ruskin with Arnold, characterizing all three as co-promoters of "the cozier, Victorian Wordsworth" (20).[17]

The Survival of the Pathetic Fallacy

Most reviewers of Pater's *Appreciations*, published in 1889, agreed that "Wordsworth" was the best essay in the book. The *Spectator* thought the "appreciation" of Wordsworth "excellent," and "full of acute remarks" (Seiler, 212), while the *Pall Mall Gazette* described the essay as abounding in "cosmic critical truths" (199). Even Mrs. Oliphant, one of Pater's severest critics, grudgingly praised the effort as a "pleasant variety upon [the] subject . . . treated with something like novelty" (219). The essay had originally appeared in *Fortnightly Review* fifteen years earlier, in 1874, under the title "On Wordsworth." This was five years before Arnold's well-known essay, at a time when Wordsworth's reputation was, for a variety of reasons, in some decline. Along with Arnold, Mill, and William Knight, Pater is responsible for Wordsworth's growing reputation in the latter part of the century.

The essay on Wordsworth was Pater's first publication after 1873's *Studies in the History of the Renaissance*, and the piece shares the polish and the abundance of metaphor that characterize those essays. Inman persuasively argues that "On Wordsworth" was originally the unpublished essay in manuscript intended for publication in *The Renaissance* but canceled by Pater in October 1872. Not only is "On Wordsworth" similar in style to the other essays in *The Renaissance*, but, Inman suggests, with the essay on Wordsworth Pater wanted to demonstrate the reappearance of the spirit of rebirth in the nineteenth century as he had with the essay on Winckelmann for the eighteenth century. Pater's comments on Wordsworth in the "Preface" are thoroughly compatible with the essay's critical approach to the poet, which is, as Inman points out, essentially an "untroubled piece of aesthetic criticism, written according to principles set down in the 'Preface'" (*Pater and His Reading*, 42).[18]

David DeLaura calls the Wordsworth essay "one of the most crucial statements of [Pater's] career," arguing that it is "his most precise attempt up to this time to define the nature of art and the nature of the perfected life" ("'Wordsworth' of Pater and Arnold," 651–52). DeLaura reads Pater's essay in relation to Arnold, in particular the latter's 1867 farewell lecture as professor of poetry at Oxford, later published in *Culture and Anarchy* as "Sweetness and Light." DeLaura argues that Pater's "ideal of 'contemplation—*being* as distinct from *doing*—a certain disposition of mind'" derives from Arnold's ideal of disinterestedness but empties Arnold's ideal of any social obligation. "Pater's 'sum of perfection in the world' has very little of the social intention of Arnold's concern for the 'volume of the human stream' sweeping toward perfection" ("'Wordsworth' of Pater and Arnold," 655). Pater's essay clearly engages and revises the professor of poetry's "study of perfection," but it is an even more radical revision of the cultural ideal of the professor of fine art, John Ruskin. We might say that in his revision of Arnold, Pater creates a most decisive alternative to Ruskin's historical and ethical framework, especially to his vision of modernity and the role of art in modern life.

Pater begins the essay by invoking "English critics at the beginning of the present century" ("On Wordsworth," 455) who sought to distinguish between the poetical faculties of the Fancy and the Imagination. He is referring to Coleridge, Leigh Hunt, and, of course, Wordsworth himself. Ruskin, too, had made much of the distinction between Imagination and Fancy; in *Modern Painters II* he uses it as the basis for the more important distinction he attempts among three forms of imagination.[19] But Ruskin disparaged the work done on the subject by what he terms "metaphysicians."[20] In contrast, Pater faults not philosophers or metaphysicians, but the ill-informed amateurs of the Victorian century who inexpertly applied the insights of German idealism:

> This metaphysical distinction, borrowed originally from the writings of German philosophers, and perhaps not always clearly apprehended by those who talked of it, involved a far deeper and more vital distinction, with which indeed all true criticism more or less directly has to do, the distinction namely between higher and lower degrees of intensity in the poet's perception of his subject, and in his concentration of himself upon his work. ("On Wordsworth," 455)

This "far deeper and more vital distinction" is the real subject of Pater's essay on Wordsworth. In his support for and expansion of the metaphysicians' distinctions, Pater directly reverses the theoretical thrust of all of Ruskin's work and especially the history of landscape art that makes up the second half of *Modern Painters III*.

Pater's endorsement of the poet's "concentration of himself" upon his act of seeing is a distinct challenge to the Victorian prose-prophets Carlyle, Arnold, Mill, and Ruskin, each of whom resists excessive self-consciousness. For Pater no profound poetry is possible without an intensity of self-consciousness. Moreover, by placing the representation of the poet's unique sensation at the heart of his theory of poetry, Pater implicitly rejects Ruskin's best-known literary concept, the pathetic fallacy. The demotion of the "Reflective or Perceptive" poet to a "second order," as Ruskin puts it, becomes a theoretical impossibility in Pater's poetics.

Pater explicitly challenges Ruskin in his choice of Wordsworth as the central poet of the modern period. In *Modern Painters III*, Ruskin had chosen Scott over Wordsworth as the "great representative of the

mind of the age in literature" (5:330). Although Wordsworth possessed "intense penetrative depth," he was guilty of hubris and affecta-
tion: "I am afraid Wordsworth was often affected in his simplicity"
(5:332). In contrast, Pater's Wordsworth is simple and unaffected; instead of "jealousy and self-complacency" (5:332) he manifests a "certain
contentment, a sort of religious placidity" ("On Wordsworth," 457).
His personality resembles that of "early Italian or Flemish painters,
who, just because their minds were full of heavenly visions, passed,
some of them, the better part of sixty years in quiet, systematic indus-
try" (457).

More important, however, Wordsworth's unusually intense perception of the anima or soul of the natural world makes him for Pater
the central, representative poet of the age. The modern mind, according to Pater, possesses an instinctive sense of a life or spirit in nature,
and this sense is reflected in the best modern art and literature. He
speaks of an "intimate consciousness of the expression of natural
things, which weighs, listens, penetrates, where the earlier mind
passed roughly by." This evolutionary notion culminates in what he
terms "a singular chapter in the history of the human mind, [whose]
growth might be traced from Rousseau to Chateaubriand, from
Chateaubriand to Victor Hugo. . . . [I]t makes as much difference between ancient and modern landscape, as there is between the rough
masks of any early mosaic and a portrait by Reynolds or Gainsbor-
ough" (456–57).

Pater's reference to "ancient and modern landscape" undoubtedly
finds its source in Ruskin's extended discussion of the history of landscape art in *Modern Painters III*. His description of this "singular chapter" echoes Ruskin's description of the effect of landscape on the
modern as opposed to the classical and medieval mind. "The simple
fact, that we are, in some strange way, different from all the great races
that have existed before us," Ruskin writes in the chapter "Of the Novelty of Landscape,"

cannot at once be received as the proof of our own greatness; nor can it be granted, without any question, that we have a legitimate subject of complacency in being under the influence of feelings with which neither Miltiades nor the Black Prince, neither Homer nor Dante, neither Socrates nor St. Francis, could for an instant have sympathised. (5:196)

Where Ruskin asserts that in the modern period humankind has developed feelings for landscape never experienced before, however, Pater argues that the distinction between the modern sensibility and that of the past is one of degree rather than kind. An "intimate consciousness of the expression of natural things," Pater writes, "has doubtless some latent connexion with those pantheistic theories which have largely exercised men's minds in some modern systems of philosophy" ("On Wordsworth," 456–57). But there is more to the modern poetic consciousness than merely a latent connection to the past. The distinguishing feature of the modern sensibility is refinement.

Wordsworth's sensibility represents, for Pater, a continuity with the past, a "survival,"

> of that primitive condition, which some philosophers have traced in the history of human culture, in which all outward objects alike, even the works of men's hands, were believed to be endowed with life and animation, and the world was full of souls; that mood in which the old Greek gods were first begotten, and which had many strange aftergrowths. ("On Wordsworth," 458)

Pater appropriates the term "survival" from the Oxford anthropologist Edward Tylor and his 1871 study, *Primitive Culture*.[21] Tylor connects "survivals" with "animism," arguing that the belief about souls in objects, which appears throughout human cultures, can be traced from traditions of animism (Inman, *Pater and His Reading*, 57–58). In the first chapter of *Primitive Culture* Tylor defines "survivals" as

> processes, customs, opinions, and so forth, which have been car-
> ried on by force of habit into a new state of society different
> from that in which they had their original home, and they thus
> remain as proofs and examples of an older condition of culture
> out of which a newer has been evolved. (16)

For Pater, then, modern literature embodies a historically recurrent form of animism. In effect, Wordsworth's poetry is the evolutionary product of that condition, or mood, in which the old Greek gods were first begotten. And as such, Wordsworth's poetry serves as a reminder, or proof, of Greek culture.

Pater rehearses this account of animism's evolutionary recurrence in the late *Plato and Platonism*, where he figures Platonic transcenden-talism as a "recrudescence of polytheism . . . a return of the many gods of Homer, veiled now as abstract notions" (168). To the "modern an-thropologist" the Platonic theory is "but a form of what he calls 'ani-mism'":

> Animism, that tendency to locate the movements of a soul like
> our own in every object, almost in every circumstance, which
> impresses one with a sense of power, is a condition of mind, of
> which the simplest illustration is a primitive man adoring, as a
> divine being endowed with will, the meteoric stone that came
> rushing from the sky. That condition "survives" however, in the
> negro, who thinks the discharging gun a living creature; as it
> survives also, more subtly, in the culture of Wordsworth and
> Shelley, for whom clouds and peaks are kindred spirits; in the
> pantheism of Goethe; and in Schelling, who formulates that
> pantheism as a philosophic, a Platonic, theory. (169)

Pater uses a variety of rebirth images as metaphors of historical process (Shuter, "History as Palingenesis," 413). Here Pater turns to the language of modern anthropology and the notion of survival to expressively connect Platonic transcendentalism to spiritual developments of both the past and the future. In other passages, Pater exploits the language of metempsychosis, the rebirth or passage of the soul from one body to another, or the related concept of palingenesis he found in Hegel already assimilated to ideas of cultural development. As William Shuter (among others) demonstrates, Pater follows Hegel by conceiving "all historical change as part of the continuous evolutionary growth of the human spirit" ("History as Palingenesis," 414).[22]

I am arguing that in "Wordsworth" Pater rejects the plot of Ruskin's historical narrative and replaces the myth of the fall with a myth of return and refinement. Pater emphasizes the continuity of the animistic instinct without a baleful Ruskinian gap or discontinuity. Consistent with his idea of historical development, in the Wordsworth essay Pater's myth of return is an evolutionary concept proceeding from *belief* in ancient culture to *sensuous perception* in modern times:

> In the early ages this belief, delightful as its effects in poetry often are, was but the result of a crude intelligence. But in Wordsworth this power of seeing life, this perception of a soul, in inanimate things, came of an exceptional susceptibility to the impressions of eye and ear, and was at bottom a kind of sensuousness. ("On Wordsworth," 458)

To Ruskin, the slide from belief to sensuousness is precisely the flaw of modern romantic art. The absence of belief underscores the discontinuity Ruskin harps on throughout the second half of *Modern Painters III*: the pathetic fallacy is the most striking evidence of the modern poet's abuse of perception.

At this point we need to step back and remember that Ruskin does not oppose personifying landscapes. He is pleased, for instance, with the "fallacy of wilful fancy," and gives as an example Oliver Wendell Holmes's description of the crocus as a naked and shivering spendthrift. The image "involves no real expectation that it will be believed" (5:205) and Ruskin tells us that his favorite poems are full of that kind of figuration. The real subject of his inquiry is that "fallacy caused by an excited state of the feelings, making us, for the time, more or less irrational" (5:205). This is the pathetic fallacy, the indulgence of the second-order reflective poet. But Ruskin is pleased by many of these figures as well, including the famous example he gives from Kingsley's *Alton Locke*,

> They rowed her in across the rolling foam—
> The cruel, crawling foam.

Ruskin deems Kingsley's expression of feeling sincere. He is pleased with the lines "not because they fallaciously describe foam, but because they faithfully describe sorrow. But the moment the mind of the speaker becomes cold, that moment every such expression becomes untrue, as being for ever untrue in the external facts" (5:210–11). For Ruskin, like Wordsworth, there is no baser poetical habit than using metaphorical expressions in cold blood. Nevertheless, even when the pathetic fallacy results from heartfelt emotion it is "for ever untrue in the external fact" and is for this reason an indulgence of the second-order poet.

Distortion of external fact, Ruskin notoriously argues, results from an absence or breakdown of self-control. Modern poetry lacks restraint and so permits the passions of a moment to alter nature. Ruskin finds the modern romantic poet guilty of a kind of poetic insubordination characterized by pride and self-indulgence. The full force and vehemence of Ruskin's charge is not evident until chapter 16 of *Modern Painters III*, "Of Modern Landscape," where he compares Scott to other modern poets, particularly Wordsworth. I will take up that part of Ruskin's argument in the next section.

At this stage, however, I would like to address another component of Ruskin's charge—that the pathetic fallacy is a sign of disbelief. In chapter 13, "Of Classical Landscape," Ruskin distinguishes the pathetic fallacy, "eminently characteristic of the modern mind" (5:221), from the landscape personifications of the classical world, specifically represented by Homer. The distinction turns on faith. According to Ruskin, the classical poet attributes his sense of animation in nature to the gods. His feeling that "the sea-wave appeared wayward or idle" reflects the mood of the "Great Water Spirit" (5:224) who inhabits the water much as an immortal soul inhabits the body. Homer's separation of the sea from the Sea Power signals to Ruskin Homer's belief in a deity and, more to the point, proves that Homer never confuses the salt water with the deity that animates the water. In contrast, the modern poet reflects his culture's "general profanity of temper" regarding nature, "a total absence of faith in the presence of any deity therein" (5:320). The absence of faith leads to confusion regarding the natural world and the habitual replacement of divine spirit with the projection of human emotion. With the ancients, Ruskin argues,

> when Diana is said to hunt with her nymphs in the woods, it does not mean merely, as Wordsworth puts it, that the poet or shepherd saw the moon and stars glancing between the branches of the trees, and wished to say so figuratively. It means that there is a living spirit, to which the light of the moon is a body; which takes delight in glancing between the clouds and following the wild beasts as they wander through the night. (5:227)

For Ruskin, the pathetic fallacy reflects an immense gap between Homer and Wordsworth, a fall from faith to sensuousness.

Of course, we should not forget the ambiguity in the pathetic fallacy. Ruskin's point in "The Moral of Landscape," the last chapter in his history of landscape art, is that while the fallacy reflects the moral degradation and absence of belief in modern life, the preoccupation with the animation of landscape is the surest route back to genuine belief (Bate, 62–85). The gap is wide, but Ruskin holds open the possibility of a return to God. We should also note that, as his comments on Greek religion suggest, his idea of faith at this point in his life extends far beyond evangelical Christianity.

In addressing the pathetic fallacy—as so often in his responses to Ruskin's ideas—Pater shifts the grounds of discussion. His glorification of the refined sensuousness of the modern poet leads us to infer that he would characterize Homer's putative separation of the sea from the Sea Power as the manifestation of a cruder sensibility. By stressing the continuity of the animistic instinct, Pater erases the stigma of the pathetic fallacy. He insists on its familiarity as a component of poetry from time immemorial, and he obdurately refuses to make a distinction like Ruskin's between a so-called healthy Homeric myth and a faithless modern myth. Instead, he characterizes the transition between phases as a modern survival of animism more subtle than earlier recurrences because it represents a more conscious phase in its evolution. Pater's modern romantic artists—Wordsworth and Rossetti and Leonardo and Michelangelo—are architects of genuine myth. They create allegorical figures that breathe with life, partly figurative and partly literal.

The Power of Pathos

One of Ruskin's oddest judgments is that Walter Scott is the representative poet of his age. As the representative modern poet, Scott shares the faults and weaknesses of his age—its faithlessness, its lack of aesthetic principles, its strange interweaving of levity and melancholy. But Scott most successfully resists the pernicious tendencies of his time. He stands as an exception to the characteristic weakness of the modern intelligence, for he does not rely upon the pathetic fallacy.[23] Scott is ultimately able

> to conquer all tendencies to the pathetic fallacy, and, instead of making Nature anywise subordinate to himself, he makes him-

> self subordinate to *her*—follows her lead simply—does not ven-
> ture to bring his own cares and thoughts into her pure and quiet
> presence—paints her in her simple and universal truth, adding
> no result of momentary passion or fancy, and appears, therefore,
> at first shallower than other poets, being in reality wider and
> healthier. (5:342–43)

Scott is an exception among modern artists. "All the rest," Ruskin
complains, "carry their cares to [Nature], and begin maundering in her
ears about their own affairs" (5:343). Tennyson, Keats, Byron, and
Shelley exhibit either a lack of "real sympathy" with nature, or a "trou-
blesome selfishness."

> Wordsworth is more like Scott, and understands how to be
> happy, but yet cannot altogether rid himself of the sense that he
> is a philosopher, and ought always to be saying something wise.
> He has also a vague notion that nature would not be able to get
> on well without Wordsworth; and finds a considerable part of
> his pleasure in looking at himself as well as at her. But with
> Scott the love is entirely humble and unselfish. (5:343)

Scott's habit of looking at nature is not altered by his own feelings.
Rather, he regards nature "as having an animation and pathos of *its
own*, wholly irrespective of human presence or passion" (5:340).[24]

Ruskin begs his own question here, and this is always the critical
problem in understanding his formulation of the fallacy. How is the
claim that nature has a pathos of its own somehow less pathetic and
less fallacious than Coleridge's dancing leaf or Kingsley's crawling
foam? But that is the question of an unbeliever. For Ruskin regarded
the beauty of the natural world as a gift from God, and so the apprehension of beauty is the apprehension of divine qualities and fulfills
what is most God-like in man.

Pater never mentions Scott in the Wordsworth essay, but he does
conspicuously refer to him, two years later, as a poet who has been

incorrectly labeled "romantic."[25] To Pater, Scott does not represent the romantic spirit because of the absence in his work of distortion grounded in emotion. Pater deems Wordsworth the representative poet of his age precisely because he demonstrates, better than any other modern poet, the relation between the human mind and nature.

> In the airy building of the brain, a special day or hour even, comes to have for him a sort of personal identity, a spirit or angel given to it, by which, for its exceptional insight, or the happy light upon it, it has a presence in one's history, and acts there, as a separate power or accomplishment; and he has celebrated in many of his poems the "efficacious spirit," which, as he says, resides in these "particular spots" of time. ("On Wordsworth," 458)

The passage is a beautiful paraphrase of the famous passage in *The Prelude*, "There are in our existence spots of time." By directly quoting "efficacious spirit" Pater calls special attention to these lines from the poem.

> This efficacious spirit chiefly lurks
> Among those passages of life that give
> Profoundest knowledge to what point, and how,
> The mind is lord and master—outward sense
> The obedient servant of her will.
>
> (XII, 219–23)

Ruskin's avoidance of *The Prelude* looks even more conspicuous in light of Pater's more than fifteen references to the autobiographical poem. Pater transforms what Ruskin deems Wordsworth's greatest liability—the mind as "lord and master"—into the poet's greatest strength.

Moreover, even in his description of Wordsworth's power to see into the life of things, Pater's choice of words and images actually

evokes Ruskin's chapter on the pathetic fallacy. He describes a
Wordsworth who is unable to distinguish between the animate and
the inanimate, for everything breathes with life.

> That sense of a life in natural objects, which in most poetry is
> only a rhetorical artifice, is in Wordsworth the assertion of what
> for him is almost literal fact. To him every natural object seemed
> to possess more or less of a moral or spiritual life. . . . An ema-
> nation, a particular spirit, belonged, not to the moving leaves or
> water only, but to the distant peak arising suddenly by some
> change of perspective above the nearer horizon. ("On Words-
> worth," 458)

Of the hundreds of images in Wordsworth that express a sense of life
in natural things, Pater chooses to echo Ruskin's specific illustrations
of the pathetic fallacy, Kingsley's crawling foam and Coleridge's dancing leaf.

Wordsworth's depictions of country life are characterized by what
Pater calls a "penetrative pathos," a quality that places the poet among
those "masters of the sentiment of pity in literature" (460). Pater will
later attribute the "sentiment of pity" to such artists as Michelangelo,
Botticelli, and his own fictional characters Marius, Gaston, and Florian Deleal. This instinctive pathos allows Wordsworth, like Florian,
to sympathize with all aspects of the pastoral world, "the sorrows of
the wild creatures even, their home-sickness, their strange yearnings"
(460). By collecting "all the traces of vivid excitement" (460) in the
pastoral world, Wordsworth conveys the sense of "passionate regret"
that is associated with "a ruined farm-building, a heap of stones, a deserted sheepfold" (460); he depicts the "pathetic wanness" of those
who have been wronged,

> all the pathetic episodes of their humble existence, their long-
> ing, their wonder at fortune, their poor pathetic pleasures, like

the pleasures of children, won so hardly in the struggle for bare existence, their yearning towards each other in their darkened houses, or at their early toil. (460)

Pater's sudden and repeated use of the word "pathetic" signals his dramatic reversal of Ruskin's fallacy. Coming in the midst of his celebration of the pathetic fallacy as it reaches its highest and most profound expression with Wordsworth, the repeated use of the adjective strongly suggests an engagement with Ruskin.

Pater finds an amplification in Wordsworth's pathos leading to dignity. The poet is instinctively drawn to "people from humble life," provincial people whose lives are spent, generation after generation, in the "same abiding place." The attachment to "actual scenes and places" produces a strong "religious sentiment."

> Consisting, as it did so much, in the recognition of local sanctities, in the habit of connecting the stones and trees of a particular spot of earth with the great events of life, till the low walls, the green mounds, the half-obliterated epitaphs seemed full of voices and a sort of natural oracles, the very religion of these people of the dales seemed but another link between them and the earth, and was literally a religion of nature. (459)

This sincere religious emotion gives to peasant life a certain composure and stateliness, a "natural dignity." In *Marius the Epicurean*, Pater associates this same kind of simplicity with the ancient Roman religion of Numa. As William Shuter recognizes, what "Pater calls 'the religion of Numa' is the Roman equivalent of the chthonic religions of primitive Greece" ("History as Palingenesis," 418). It might be argued that, for Pater, Wordsworth's reverence for country life is the modern equivalent of the chthonic instinct.

In his depictions of common life, Pater's Wordsworth achieves a "passionate sincerity," and thereby "indirectly" makes an appeal "for that sincerity, that perfect fidelity to one's own inward presentations, to the precise feature of the picture within" ("On Wordsworth," 459).

For Pater, it is the poet's profound and determined pursuit of the picture within that leads him into "bold trains of speculative thought" (461). The ceaseless workings of the human mind, the constant drift of momentary impressions and observations, a "chance expression . . . placed in a new connection," or a "sudden memory of a thing long past" (461), becomes for him the promise of a future life, and support for the ancient doctrine of metempsychosis.

> Following the soul backwards and forwards on these endless ways, his sense of man's dim, potential powers became a pledge to him, indeed, of a future life; but carried him back also to that mysterious notion of an earlier state of existence, the fancy of the Platonists, the old heresy of Origen. (461)

In this language, we recognize not only the ancient doctrine of metempsychosis, but also Pater's more modern anthropological interest in survival. As Robert Crawford points out, in the Wordsworth essay "[a]nthropology and aestheticism merge" (874). Pater's yoking of the literary and the anthropological within the background of palingenesis and metempsychosis characterizes both his appreciation of Wordsworth and his philosophical critique of Ruskin.

Pater identifies the "Intimations" ode as the crucial expression of Wordsworth's bold speculative thought, the point at which the poet comes "into strange contact" with these exotic thoughts from the past. Representing the philosophy of the ode as consistent with a permanent tendency of human thought, as he had with Wordsworth's instinct toward the perception of life in natural objects, Pater situates the ode within a philosophical tradition going back to Plato's *Phaedo* (Inman, *Pater and His Reading*, 63).

> It was in this mood that he conceived those oft-reiterated regrets for a half-ideal childhood, when the relics of Paradise still clung about the soul—a childhood, as it seemed, full of the fruits of old age, lost for all in a degree in the passing away of the youth of the world, lost for each over again in the passing away

of actual youth. It is this ideal childhood which he celebrates in his famous "Ode on the Recollections of Childhood," and some other poems which may be grouped around it, like the lines on "Tintern Abbey." ("On Wordsworth," 461)

As I noted earlier, Ruskin complained that the mature mind held no compensation equivalent to the early perceptive powers of childhood. Pater does not seem to be as exercised by this kind of loss largely because he sees a fluent recurrence where Ruskin sees uncompensated absence.

Ruskin, of course, fears the dangerous potential of the mind to create a world of only its own making, a world stripped of social responsibility. Pater, too, acknowledges the dangers of Wordsworth's philosophic imagination, the tendency toward an extreme solipsism. In the midst of the poet's "moments of profound, imaginative power" there lurk frightening destructive forces. But Wordsworth's spots of time are triumphs of the isolated consciousness, testament to the imagination's power to shape form from formlessness. Anticipating the famous passage in the Giorgione essay, Pater describes Wordsworth's poetry as uniting

> with absolute justice the word and the idea, each in the imaginative flame becoming inseparably one with the other, by that fusion of matter and form which is the characteristic of the highest poetical expression. His words are themselves thought and feeling; not eloquent or musical words merely, but that sort of creative language which carries the reality of what it depicts directly, to the consciousness. ("On Wordsworth," 463)

J. P. Ward has suggested that with the phrase, "words are themselves thought and feeling," Pater has joined Arnold, Coleridge, Mill, and Harriet Martineau as Victorian critics who, with similar one-phrase judgments of the poet, "underline, and with approval, the simple and even poetically negative quality of Wordsworth's poetry" (Ward, 64).[26]

But Pater's comments on Wordsworth's style hardly suggest a poet of negative quality. Instead, Wordsworth's diction is artistically faultless, for the word is united with the idea, "which is the characteristic of the highest poetical expression." "All the laws of good writing," Pater writes in the 1888 essay "Style," "aim at a . . . unity or identity of the mind in all the processes by which the word is associated to its import. The term is right, and has its essential beauty, when it becomes, in a manner, what it signifies, as with the names of simple sensations" (*Appreciations*, 22). The highest poetical expression is characterized by the sensuous illustration of the individual "apprehending mind."

Being and Doing

In the most provocative section of the Wordsworth essay, Pater introduces a controversial theme drawn straight out of the pages of the Renaissance Humanists. "That the end of life," he asserts, "is not action but contemplation, *being* as distinct from *doing*, a certain disposition of the mind, is in some shape or other the principle of all the higher morality" ("On Wordsworth," 465). The humanist debate, while of course unresolved, pitted the *vita activa* against the *vita contemplativa*, generally classifying poetry as a product of the contemplative life that nevertheless moved human beings to noble action. But Pater seems expressly to avoid such a notion of poetry. In his view, Wordsworth and the ancients are experts in "impassioned art":

> Their work is, not to teach lessons, or enforce rules, or even to stimulate us to noble ends, but to withdraw the thoughts for a little while from the mere machinery of life, to fix them with appropriate emotions on the spectacle of those great facts in man's existence which no machinery affects. (465)

It is difficult to believe that Pater's ideal of poetry includes no didactic component or even an element of stimulation to noble ends, particularly since he speaks elsewhere of poetry's moral significance. Yet this extreme doctrine, perhaps best labeled aestheticism, has distinct power as a refutation of Ruskin's ideal of the poet's social responsibility. As I have noticed elsewhere, Ruskin himself lays the foundations of this aesthetic approach (Daley, "From Theoretic to Practical"). But Pater's extremism—seen, perhaps, in his wholesale distortion of the Renaissance debate—allows him to contravene Ruskin with the tools Ruskin supplied.

The Wordsworth essay originally was meant to conclude *The Renaissance*. It is not accidental that Pater deliberately distorts Renaissance poetics while alluding to the humanist debate on the artistic and contemplative life. Indeed, the Renaissance humanists themselves are analogous to Ruskin in furnishing Pater with the language and themes from which he will derive a new discourse and a new Renaissance.

Two ❧ Romanticism and the Italian Renaissance

T HE publication in 1873 of *Studies in the History of the Renaissance* marked the most significant treatment in English of the Italian Renaissance since Ruskin's *The Stones of Venice*.[1] As the greatest and most famous English critic of the visual arts, Ruskin was the inescapable point of comparison for readers and reviewers of Pater's new book. "Modern art-criticism," wrote William Dean Howells, reviewing *The Renaissance* for the *Atlantic Monthly*,

> is attributive when it supposes itself interpretive. The sight of an old painting inspires the critic with certain emotions, and these he straightway seizes upon as the motive of the painter. It *may* happen that both are identical; or it may happen that the effect produced was never in the painter's mind at all. Very likely it was not; but this vice, which Mr. Ruskin invented, goes on perpetuating itself; and Mr. Pater, who is as far from thinking with Mr. Ruskin as from writing like him, falls a helpless prey to it. (Seiler, 21)

A number of critics cited Ruskin as the foundation of Pater's "impressionistic" or "aesthetic" criticism, including Mrs. Oliphant, W. J.

Courthope, and John Morley, who, with his article in the *Fortnightly Review*, describes Ruskin as the first in a line of "aesthetic spirits" who turned to art as a substitute for religion.

> Then Mr. Ruskin came, and the Pre-Raphaelite painters, and Mr. Swinburne, and Mr. Morris, and now lastly a critic like Mr. Pater, all with faces averted from theology, most of them indeed blessed with a simple and happy unconsciousness of the very existence of the conventional gods. (Seiler, 69)

T. S. Eliot later replaces Ruskin with Arnold in this list, but the sense that Pater's association of moral character with aesthetic sensibility originated somehow with Ruskin was palpable to many among the book's initial audience.

Equally apparent, as the passage from Howell's review suggests, were the vast differences between the two critics. Pater's refined and suggestive style was in stark contrast to the more ardent rhetoric of Ruskin's many books and lectures. Pater was accused of pretension and superficiality. His use of the word "pulsations" reminds an anonymous reviewer in the *Examiner* of Dickens's scathing portrait of Leigh Hunt.

> The very word itself recalls Mr. Harold Skimpole. If utilitarianism had no value of its own, it would yet be valuable as a protest against this new "lilies of the field" theory of life and its duties. Mr. Ruskin is as fond of art and gets as many "pulsations" out of it as most men. We should like to know his opinion of Mr. Pater and of Mr. Pater's critic. (Seiler, 77)

Most importantly, critics explicitly noted that Pater's view of the Renaissance differed sharply from Ruskin's condemnation of the period.

> It is curious that having much of the dogmatism, inaccuracy, fancifulness, love of paradox, and arbitrariness of Ruskin, Mr.

Pater's purpose should be the glorification of that period or movement, as one may consider it, which has called forth the former's most eloquent denunciations. (Seiler, 99)

Sidney Colvin, Slade Professor of Fine Art at Cambridge, emphasized Pater's rejection of Ruskin's more accepted view of a discontinuity between the Middle Ages and the Renaissance. He praised Pater's rejection of conventional historical boundaries:

> Another notion of the Renaissance prevails, representing it as a movement of discontinuity, a movement of aggression and innovation, whereby Pagan thought and Pagan art were enthroned, and Christian art supplanted or brought low. It was from writers of the modern Catholic school in France, and most of all from the eloquent and comprehensive work of Rio, that this notion got hold of us. . . . The writers in England, who approached with most enthusiasm the history of art, failed to perceive that . . . Middle Age and Renaissance presented in reality successive phases of an unbroken movement of the human spirit, a gathering curiosity about the universe and the past, a gathering desire to really live, feel, and know. Failing to perceive this, those writers were content to take over the notions of Rio and the Catholic School, and to enforce and develop them with new vehemence and acuteness, until they had got to rule the popular mind. (Seiler, 48)

Although he never mentions Ruskin by name, Colvin is undoubtedly referring to him when he alludes to "writers in England" possessing the "most enthusiasm" for the history of art, and failing to perceive the continuity between the Middle Age and Renaissance. That Ruskin had enthusiastically embraced "the notions of Rio" was common knowledge. In opposition, Pater identified with Rio's antagonist, Michelet. For many English admirers of Italian art, Pater's depiction of the Renaissance was a welcome alternative to Ruskin.

Ruskin's Renaissance

For Ruskin, the destructive forces of the Renaissance extend into the nineteenth century, "from the Grand Canal to Gower Street" (11:4). The plot of Ruskin's historical narrative is well known. Once the "Renaissance frosts came . . . all perished" (11:22), and the story of the death of Venice is meant to inspire nothing less than a nineteenth-century resurrection of Gothic culture and feeling. Renaissance pride and infidelity destroy the "great Gothic spirit"—an exuberant energy characterized by imperfection and represented in images of the organic, ever-changing natural world. Ruskin's Gothic is as much the spirit of an ideal romanticism as it is "the spirit of an ideal Christianity" (Sawyer, 115).

The aim of *The Stones of Venice* is to encourage a revival of Gothic architecture as a means of resuscitating the "great Gothic spirit." Ruskin identifies landscape painting as a "healthy effort to fill the void which the destruction of Gothic architecture has left." But landscape painting ultimately fails, in his view, to influence the masses:

> The art of landscape-painting will never become thoroughly interesting or sufficing to the minds of men engaged in active life, or concerned principally with practical subjects. The sentiment and imagination necessary to enter fully into the romantic forms of art are chiefly the characteristics of youth; so that nearly all men as they advance in years, and some even from their childhood upwards, must be appealed to, if at all, by the direct and substantial art, brought before their daily observation and connected with their daily interests. No form of art answers these conditions so well as architecture. (11:226)

Several of Ruskin's favorite hobby horses appear in this passage: the active life, the (lower case) romantic forms of art, and the instinct of childhood. Further, Ruskin is here palpably the social critic urging the utility of art as a valuable contribution to the active and the practical life. Therefore, he can claim that the "romantic" art of painting is not as effective as the more "substantial" art of architecture, where "effective" means both reaching and influencing the largest number of people.

The paradox of Ruskin's assertion regarding Gothic architecture is that romantic forms of art (i.e., painting) are not in themselves adequate to produce what he considers the true romantic feeling of the Goth. Thus, for Ruskin modern art falls short of medieval art in that its putative romanticism constitutes a degradation of this true romantic feeling.

For Ruskin, the "romantic" is never a rigorous concept. It is best understood as analogous to the Gothic, not necessarily in the six characteristic elements, but rather in association with the more nebulous qualities of passion, nobility, and franchise. The last of these Ruskin describes as an idealized form of individual liberty. Ruskin makes explicit the connection between the romantic and Gothic franchise only in his 1873 Oxford lecture "Franchise," but it informs his moral history of Venice and the discontinuity between Gothic and Renaissance.

Ruskin values the synthesizing power of the Gothic imagination in its fusion of disparate architectural styles. The Venetian Gothic is a historical symbol of one such imaginative triumph.

> Opposite in their character and mission, alike in their magnificence of energy, they came from the North and from the South, the glacier torrent and the lava stream: they met and contended over the wreck of the Roman empire; and the very centre of the struggle, the point of pause of both, the dead water of the opposite eddies, charged with embayed fragments of the Roman wreck, is VENICE. The Ducal palace of Venice contains the three elements in exactly equal proportions—the Roman, Lombard, and Arab. It is the central building of the world. (9:38)

Putting aside the fantasy of "exactly equal proportions," we find in this passage a good example of Ruskin's admiration for what Coleridge calls the "esemplastic" power. Ruskin makes much use of Coleridge's organic analogies in his description of the assimilating powers of the imagination. He brings Venetian architecture to life with an abundance of organic imagery (Gurewitsch). Like Coleridge and other philosophers of romanticism, Ruskin internalizes the syncretic attributes of Gothic architecture and by sheer force of imagination transforms chaos into harmony. In the last volume of *Stones*, however, he warns that the force of imagination can lead to a kind of artistic narcissism.

Ruskin's Renaissance is the Gothic gone bad. The fall of Venice results from a perversion of the Gothic imagination. The Renaissance represents the replacement of nature with artifice, the expression of personality as the glorification of self rather than as the perception and adoration of God's world.

> For, as it is written, "He that trusteth in his own heart is a fool," so also it is written, "The fool hath said in his heart, There is no God"; and the self-adulation which influenced not less the learning of the age than its luxury, led gradually to the forgetfulness of all things but self, and to an infidelity only the more fatal because it still retained the form and language of faith. (11:120)

This is the crux of Ruskin's critique of modern romantic art. His notion of infidelity is the source of the pathetic fallacy: an infidelity that retains "the form and language of faith" is parallel to a poetry that retains the recognition of animate life without the belief in the power that animates it. Pater, for his part, rejects the very notion of dividing faith from form, or belief from the rhetoric of belief.

The bulk of Ruskin's thirty-thousand-word essay on Renaissance pride, the second chapter in volume 3 of *Stones*, is a tour of Venetian tombs and sepulchres, "conclusive" evidence of the period's pride and folly. The simplicity of the Gothic tombs, "confessing the power, and accepting the peace, of death, openly and joyfully; and in all their symbols marking that the hope of resurrection lay only in Christ's righteousness" (II:82), gives way to the ornate decoration and arrogance of the Renaissance tombs. The "mere slab of stone" that in the thirteenth century serves as the lid of the sarcophagus is replaced by "a mass of marble, sixty or seventy feet in height" (II:113); the "rude figures" of Christ and his apostles are replaced by statues of the Doges themselves, surrounded by "scattered Virtues, Victories, Fames, genii,—the entire company of the monumental stage assembled, as before a drop scene, executed by various sculptors, and deserving attentive study as exhibiting every condition of false taste and feeble conception" (II:113). The modest and unadorned epitaph of 1252, "Here lies the Lord Marin Morosini, Duke," swells to the egotistic inscription of 1547:

> "James Pesaro, Bishop of Paphos, who conquered the Turks in war, himself in peace, transported from a noble family among the Venetians to a nobler among the angels, laid here, expects the noblest crown, which the just Judge shall give to him in that day. He lived the years of Plato. He died 24th March 1547."

> The mingled classicism and carnal pride of this epitaph surely need no comment. The crown is expected as a right from the justice of the Judge, and the nobility of the Venetian family is only a little lower than that of the angels. (II:110)

The renewal of classical interest, indicated by the epitaph's allusion to Plato, Ruskin regards as both a cause and a result of Renaissance infidelity. He denounces the "fatal" Renaissance enthusiasm for classical literature. Although he will later radically revise his judgment on the relation between pagan and Christian ideals in the Renaissance, in 1853 he wholeheartedly condemns what he sees as the false and shallow reconciliation of the pagan and Christian:

> It would have been better to have worshipped Diana and Jupiter at once, than to have gone on through the whole of life naming one God, imagining another, and dreading none. (II:129–30)

He adds that the "images summoned by art began gradually to assume one average value in the spectator's mind; and incidents from the Iliad and from the Exodus to come within the same degrees of credibility" (11:130–31). This obvious denunciation of the Renaissance in relation to a fully idealized Gothic culture seems deliberately to overpolarize the nuances of symbolic representation to which Ruskin is so alert in other contexts.

Contrary to most subsequent historians, Ruskin perceives the scientific and technical achievements of the Renaissance as a deadening force, encouraging a vain desire for perfection, the loss of religious feeling, and the pursuit of selfish and sensuous pleasure. Applied to artistic production, scientific advances stifled the artist's imaginative expression. He identifies the Renaissance pride of knowledge as its "chief element of weakness," prohibiting "rudeness in expression" and so stifling human emotion. The "demand for perfection," Ruskin argues, is the "first attack of the Renaissance upon the Gothic schools" (11:15).

Ruskin draws a connection between technical advances, virtuosic displays of skill, and the period's "unscrupulous *pursuit of pleasure*" (11:135). Renaissance art is often an expression of "inordinate play," an unhealthy and excessive "spirit of jesting" (11:136). In his chapter "Grotesque Renaissance," Ruskin describes this "spirit of idiotic mockery" as the "most striking characteristic of the last period of the Renaissance" (11:145). Ruskin's argument here is composed of an almost endless number of distinctions and classifications, and the irony of this style, coming after the attack on Renaissance system, "the curious tendency to formulization and system which . . . encumbered the minds of the Renaissance schoolmen" (11:115), is all too apparent. Nonetheless, the reader cannot misconstrue the consequence of Venetian luxury and self-indulgence.[2]

Pater's Renaissance

In its historical characteristics, Pater's Renaissance closely resembles Ruskin's. As Wendell Harris remarks, they "equally recognized the

classical influences, the surging individualism, the explicit pursuit of
pleasure, the rise of science, the growth of a class of men of refined, if
selfish and worldly aesthetic sensibilities" ("Ruskin and Pater," 175).
They "saw very much the same Renaissance while using it wholly dif-
ferently" (176). Any reader leafing through the few pages of the "Preface" quickly comprehends that Pater is putting the Renaissance to a
wholly different use. Fifteenth-century Italy "can hardly be studied too
much," Pater tells his reader,

> not merely for its positive results in the things of the intellect
> and the imagination, its concrete works of art, its special and
> prominent personalities, with their profound aesthetic charm,
> but for its general spirit and character, *for the ethical qualities of
> which it is a consummate type.* (xxiii, italics mine)[3]

Rather than a type of moral degeneration, the Renaissance embodies
a positive ethos of intellectual curiosity and sympathy, a "spirit of general elevation and enlightenment" (xxiv).

For Pater, this humanistic spirit is readily discernible in the age
preceding the fifteenth century, repudiating Ruskin's notion of the
Renaissance as a massive rupture with the past. As in his account of
modern poetry's animistic instinct, we see Pater's emphasis on continuity, on survival, on steady recurrence.

> This outbreak of the human spirit may be traced far into the
> middle age itself, with its motives already clearly pronounced,
> the care for physical beauty, the worship of the body, the break-
> ing down of those limits which the religious system of the middle
> age imposed on the heart and the imagination. (xxii–xxiii)[4]

In his *Hebrew and Hellene in Victorian England*, DeLaura reads this passage as a "direct denial of Arnold's praise of the Middle Ages as the
supreme era of 'the heart and imagination'" (243). The phrase "heart
and imagination" is clearly adopted from Arnold's 1864 Oxford lecture
"Pagan and Medieval Religious Sentiment," but Pater's sentiment is as

easily directed against Ruskin, whose praise of Gothic heart and imagination is far more extreme than Arnold's. Arnold's ideal is, of course, the "imaginative reason," which represents the reconciliation of St. Francis and Theocritus, the medieval "heart and imagination" with the pagan "senses and understanding." Pater locates that reconciliation, as DeLaura notes, in the Renaissance, while Arnold finds it in fifth-century Greek poetry. Pater's endorsement of "earthy passion" and "worship of the body," however, is no more a part of Arnold's ideal Greece than it is of Ruskin's ideal Middle Age.

Pater discerns one continuous movement of the human spirit from the Middle Ages through the Renaissance and into modern life. Works of art, Pater suggests, are the means of grasping the continuity from one age to the next, and so included in Pater's Renaissance are "two little compositions in early French," as well as the mid-sixteenth-century French poetry of Joachim du Bellay and the eighteenth-century writing of Winckelmann.

In relation to continuity, reconciliation is one of Pater's primary themes. In *The Renaissance*, observes U. C. Knoepflmacher, "the imagistic emphasis on the fluidity of water and music contributes to our belief in the flow of a movement that can supersede all differences between periods, types, temperaments, nationalities, and forms. Opposites dissolve" ("Arnold's Fancy," 105; Stein, 225). Not only is the Renaissance a continuation of the Middle Age, but what Ruskin sees as a false and hypocritical attempt at reconciliation between pagan and Christian is, for Pater, merely the inspired result of the humanistic Renaissance spirit. The revival of classical antiquity in the fifteenth century "was only one of many results of a general excitement and enlightening of the human mind, but of which the great aim and achievements of what, as Christian art, is often falsely opposed to the Renaissance, were another result" (xxii).[5] According to Pater, "Christian art" of the Middle Ages had been misrepresented by writers such as Rio, Ruskin, and Tyrwhitt. These historians had, deliberately or not, suppressed the "antinomian" characteristics of the Middle Age, its spirit of rebellion and revolt against the moral and religious ideas of the time. In their search after the pleasures of the senses and the imagination, in their care for beauty, in their worship of the body, people were impelled beyond the bounds of the Christian ideal; and their love became sometimes a strange idolatry, a strange rival religion. It was the return of that ancient Venus, not dead, but only hidden for a time in the caves of the Venusberg, of those old pagan gods still going to and fro on the earth, under all sorts of disguises. And this element in the middle age, for the most part ignored by those writers who have treated it preeminently as the "Age of Faith"—this rebellious and antinomian element, the recognition of which has made the delineation of the middle age by the writers of the Romantic school in France, by Victor Hugo for instance in *Notre-Dame de Paris*, so suggestive and exciting—is found alike in the history of Abelard and the legend of Tannhäuser. (18–19)

The pagan element had already been present in the Middle Age, serving as the complement or counterpart to the Christian spirit of the time.[6]

This "coexistence of opposites" is, as Wolfgang Iser has explained, the typical means of Paterian reconciliation.

Reconciliation was not a dialectic movement towards synthesis; it was, rather, an interaction of opposites, a telescoping of incompatibles, resulting in a syncretic and synchronic perception of what was and what had been. . . . For Pater, then, the Renaissance reconciles Christian and pagan elements by making each relative to the other as interacting appearances. (39–40)

The essays in *The Renaissance* demonstrate, again and again, this aesthetic process of reconciliation, the synchronization of opposites that grows from and helps create the Renaissance spirit of unity—the reconciliation of Renaissance sweetness and Gothic strength in the stories of "Amis and Amile," "Aucassin and Nicolette," of Hebraism and Hellenism in the strange philosophies of Pico, of the profane and sacred in the paintings of Botticelli, of Greek sculpture with the Renaissance system of Michelangelo in Luca della Robbia, of Dante and Plato in Michelangelo's own work, beauty and terror in Leonardo, form and matter in Giorgione, Gothic and Renaissance in Joachim du Bellay.

This interaction of opposites, an important characteristic of Pater's conception of any historical period, works not only to elucidate the continuities between one age and the next, but also to distinguish the spirit or *Zeitgeist* of one age from another. The Renaissance is both a "symbol of an attitude toward experience," as Wendell Harris describes it ("Ruskin and Pater," 181), and a very definite and particular historical period, possessing its own unique set of relations. "Beauty," Pater writes in the book's first paragraph,

> like all other qualities presented to human experience, is relative; and the definition of it becomes unmeaning and useless in proportion to its abstractness. To define beauty, not in the most abstract but in the most concrete terms possible, to find, not its universal formula, but the formula which expresses most adequately this or that special manifestation of it, is the aim of the true student of aesthetics. (xix)

Critics have recognized that Pater's appeal to the concrete over the abstract is, among other things, a polemical poke at Ruskin, who in *Modern Painters II* had made "elaborate efforts to define beauty in abstract terms" (Hill, 294; Inman, *Pater's Reading*, 274; Williams, 51–53).

As Carolyn Williams emphasizes, Pater's historicism "distinguishes his aestheticism from other versions of aestheticism in English" (47). She argues further that Pater's advocacy of a "heightened sense of historical difference" creates a "critical distance" from Ruskin (51–53). But given that the whole of *The Stones of Venice* consists of aesthetic evaluation based on an outrageously heightened sense of his-

torical difference, I think that Pater's theoretical Preface works to un-
dermine Ruskin's overdetermined historicism. Pater creates a critical
distance not merely from Ruskin's tendency toward the abstract, but
from his far more pervasive tendency toward the absolute, whether
that be manifested in historical concreteness, as in *Stones*, or philosophical abstractness, as in *Modern Painters II*. We can say, as indeed
Williams does, that Pater's "historicism" is far more modern than
Ruskin's, that it calls into question the very possibility of historical
knowledge itself, revealing an extreme attitude of self-consciousness.[7]

Pater's best-known substitution of the relative for the absolute is
his revision of Arnold's dictum from "The Function of Criticism at
the Present Time."

> "To see the object as in itself it really is," has been justly said to
> be the aim of all true criticism whatever; and in aesthetic criti-
> cism the first step towards seeing one's object as it really is, is to
> know one's own impression as it really is, to discriminate it, to
> realise it distinctly. (xix)

Behind Pater's explicit engagement with Arnold, however, stands the
paradoxical figure of Ruskin. Arnold first uttered his famous pro-
nouncement on the function of criticism as part of a polemic against
the current state of literary criticism in England, and Ruskin was his
primary example, the type of the modern "sentimental" reader. English
literature ranks behind that of France and Germany, Arnold argues,
for its critical instinct, exemplified by Ruskin, is warped by the presence of the sentimental spirit, "the strong tendency of English writers
to bring to the consideration of their object some individual fancy."
Arnold condemns Ruskin's reading of Homer, specifically his comments on the passage in *The Iliad* immediately following Helen's mention of her brothers as alive, when in fact they are dead.

> "The poet," says Mr. Ruskin, "has to speak of the earth in sad-
> ness; but he will not let that sadness affect or change his
> thought of it. No; though Castor and Pollux be dead, yet the

earth is our mother still,—fruitful, life-giving." This is a just specimen of that sort of application of modern sentiment to the ancients, against which a student, who wished to feel the ancients truly, cannot too resolutely defend himself. It reminds one, as, alas! so much of Mr. Ruskin's writing reminds one, of those words of the most delicate of living critics: "Comme tout genre de composition a son ecueil particulier, *celui du genre romanesque, c'est le faux.*" The reader may feel moved as he reads it; but it is not the less an example of "le faux" in criticism; it is false. . . . It is not true, as a matter of general criticism, that this kind of sentimentality, eminently modern, inspires Homer at all. "From Homer and Polygnotus I every day learn more clearly," says Goethe, "that in our life here above ground we have, properly speaking, to enact Hell."—if the student must absolutely have a keynote to the Iliad, let him take this of Goethe, and see what he can do with it; it will not, at any rate, like the tender pantheism of Mr. Ruskin, falsify for him the whole strain of Homer. (1:102)

Arnold takes Ruskin's discussion of Homer from the middle of Ruskin's chapter on the pathetic fallacy, but it is difficult to understand exactly what he has in mind. After all, it seems as if Arnold is using Ruskin as an example of someone engaging in the pathetic fallacy. If this is the case then doesn't he simultaneously denigrate his own argument by rejecting the Ruskin who writes so celebrated a denunciation of "tender pantheism" and "sentimentality"? It could be, perhaps, that Arnold doesn't believe that Ruskin lived by his own rule, but even so why call attention to the contradiction without articulating Ruskin's failing? And why attack the man even if, as Ruskin himself admitted, he often fell short of his poetic ideal?

When Pater revises Arnold's idea of the function of criticism, then, promoting the very critical temperament Arnold seeks to proscribe, his argument either consciously or merely by association defends Ruskin against Arnold's denigration of modern sentimentality.

Yet he must have associated Ruskin with Arnold's position. No one had asserted, again and again, and with as much passion and vigor as Ruskin, that the true properties of things were available to the senses, that to see the object as in itself it really is was not only a possibility but the duty of every man and woman. Pater's revision of Arnold applies with equal force to Ruskin, Arnold's representative sentimental critic.

The Hellenism of Pater and Ruskin

Pater's precocious essay "Winckelmann," published in 1867 when he was only twenty-seven years old, presents a lengthy, complex history of the artistic and intellectual spirit from the classical period through the Middle Ages and ending with modern life. The essay radically revises the historical narrative of Ruskin's *The Stones of Venice*. But "Winckelmann" is not simply a rejection of Ruskin's well-known moral histories. For Pater's delineation of a dark, anti-Apollonian aspect of Greek thought echoes Ruskin's own recent analysis in *Modern Painters V* in which Ruskin significantly revises his earlier judgments of Greek and Gothic art. Pater's essay, then, is both a critique of Ruskin's historical narrative and an endorsement of Ruskin's own revision of that narrative, a revision that becomes even more explicit in his Oxford lectures of the 1870s.

Johann Joachim Winckelmann is the fulcrum upon which Pater's history of the artistic spirit turns. Having recovered the glories of Greek life and art, Winckelmann simultaneously gives birth to the modern spirit, most fully represented by Goethe. Winckelmann himself embodies the Renaissance spirit, that spirit of intellectual curiosity and sympathy that is, for Pater, the ideal attitude toward experience. Along with Wordsworth, he represents Pater's type of the ideal temperament. Impassioned contemplation with Winckelmann, as with Wordsworth, is an "end-in-itself."

Armed with the works of Voltaire, Winckelmann enters Rome with "a sense of something grand, primeval, pagan, in the Catholic

religion" (Pater, "Winckelmann," 39). Such grandeur was represented
in the Vatican frescoes of Theology and Poetry, painted by Raphael,
which commemorate, for Pater, both the Christian and classical traditions, giving authority to the spiritual vitality of both. These same
frescoes had marked for Ruskin the nadir of Renaissance decline. Referring to *Disputation of the Sacrament* (fig. 1) and *Parnassus* (fig. 2),
Ruskin pronounced that

> from that spot, and from that hour, the intellect and the art of
> Italy date their degradation. Observe, however, the significance
> of this fact is not in the mere use of the figure of the heathen
> god to indicate the domain of poetry. Such a symbolical use had
> been made of the figures of heathen deities in the best times of
> Christian art. But it is in fact, that . . . *he elevated the creations of
> fancy on the one wall, to the same rank as the objects of faith upon the
> other*; that in deliberate, balanced opposition to the Rock of the
> Mount Zion, he reared the rock of Parnassus. . . . The doom of
> the arts of Europe went forth from that chamber. (12:148–50)[8]

Ruskin reiterated his condemnation of the Raphael frescoes in the
third volume of *Stones*: "and the Raphael who seemed sent and inspired
from heaven that he might paint Apostles and Prophets, sank at once
into powerlessness at the feet of Apollo and the Muses" (11:130). As
Inman observes, Pater seems to go "out of his way" to mention
Raphael's paintings (*Pater's Reading*, 127). The allusion to the frescoes
serves to introduce Winckelmann's conception of the Hellenic spirit,
but, more conspicuously, it marks a contrast with Ruskin by defending Raphael and his elevation of the pagan tradition to the spiritual
level of the Christian. Winckelmann's destiny, in Pater's description,
will be to substantiate the claims of this pagan tradition, to testify to
"the authority" of the Hellenic way of life.

Pater's delineation of the Greek ideal is in many ways dependent
on Winckelmann himself, who established the most influential model
of Hellenism for nineteenth-century writers. According to Winckel-

Fig. 1. Raphael, *Disputation of the Sacrament*, 1509, Stanza della Segnatura, Vatican (courtesy Alinari/Art Resource, NY)

Fig. 2. Raphael, *Parnassus*, 1510, Stanza della Segnatura, Vatican (courtesy Scala/Art Resource, NY)

mann, the perfection of Greek art consists in its balance and tranquillity and is characterized by ideals of formal simplicity and restraint (Aske, 71). This is the Hellenic model adopted by Goethe, Schiller, Hegel, Arnold, and, in part, by Pater. In the essay, Pater describes the Greek ideal as a golden and innocent stage in the history of the human temperament, the "unperplexed youth of humanity, seeing itself and satisfied" ("Winckelmann," 44). At the heart of Winckelmann's Hellenism lies an intense nostalgia for the past, and Pater's description of the Greek temperament as having found a "happy limit" of thought directly reflects this nostalgic tradition. The luminosity of ancient Greece is another commonplace of Romantic Hellenism, and Pater echoes Winckelmann, Carlyle, and of course, Matthew Arnold in his description of Hellenism as "the principle pre-eminently of intellectual light" (151; Aske, 45).

But Pater's essay complicates this characteristic nineteenth-century depiction of ancient Greece. For Pater suggests that Winckelmann's temperament prohibited him from sensing within the Hellenic spirit its apprehension of "conflict" and "evil," its consciousness of loss and "romantic sadness." As he does throughout the essay, Pater uses Winckelmann's relation to ancient culture and Renaissance art as a springboard for his own comprehensive historical analysis. Thus, he turns from Winckelmann's temperament to his own effort, following Hegel, to identify "a sort of preparation for the romantic within the limits of the Greek ideal itself" ("Winckelmann," 48). The customary view, Pater argues, "is only a partial one," for it fixes on "the sharp bright edge of high Hellenic culture, but loses sight of the sombre world across which it strikes" (42).[9]

Pater's emphasis on the darker, anti-Apollonian side of Greek religion stands as an immediate corrective to Arnold's conception of Greece as "sweetness and light," and is instead closer in spirit to the work of Victorian anthropologists like Edward Tylor or Andrew Lang, or to James Frazer and Friedrich Nietzsche, whose *Birth of Tragedy* would be published in 1872. But we need to include Ruskin in this list of revisionist writers who interpret Greece as the site of disorder and sorrow (Keefe, 66–71). Ruskin's mature conception of Greek art and mythology was already beginning to develop in *Modern Painters III* (1856), but *Modern Painters V,* published in 1860, is a far more striking departure from his earlier writing. Even more shocking is the shift in his thinking on Christian art that accompanies his reconception of the Greeks. When Pater took *Modern Painters V* out of the Queen's College Library in November 1863 he must have been stunned to read Ruskin's assertion that

> The art which, since the writings of Rio and Lord Lindsay, is specially known as "Christian," erred by pride in its denial of the animal nature of man;—and in connection with all monkish and fanatical forms of religion, by looking always to another world instead of this. It wasted its strength in visions. (7:264)

As is well known, Ruskin had already in the third volume of *Modern Painters* described the Purism of medieval Christian art as "childish" and an "indication of some degree of weakness in the mind pursuing it" (5:108). But the emphasis on weakness is far more pronounced in the volume of 1860. In contrast to the Purist ideal, Ruskin argues,

> the Greeks never shrink from horror; down to its uttermost depth, to its most appalling physical detail, they strive to sound the secrets of sorrow. For them there is no passing by on the other side, no turning away the eyes to vanity from pain. (7:274–75)

As Slade Professor of Fine Art at Oxford, Ruskin made his revisionary ideas of Greek art and its continuities a central theme of many of his lectures. In the sixth lecture of the 1870 *Lectures on Art,* simply titled "Light," Ruskin distinguishes the school of light, "which is essentially Greek, and full of sorrow," from the school of color, "essentially Gothic Christian and full of comfort and peace" (20: 140). While the way of color is taken by men whose bodies and minds resemble "the temper of well-brought-up children," the "way by light and shade is . . .

taken by men of the highest powers of thought, and most earnest desire for truth . . . seeking for light, they perceive also darkness"
(20:139–40). Ultimately, Ruskin is providing an elaborate rationale for
his exaltation of the Venetian school, which effects a union of Gothic
color and solemn Greek chiaroscuro. But the Gothic school is clearly
more primitive and incomplete, waiting upon the Greek conception of
spiritual darkness (Fitch, 615).

   Ruskin locates the foundations of the chiaroscurist aspect of
Greek art in Greek religion. He stresses that

> [t]he school of light is founded in the Doric worship of Apollo,
> and the Ionic worship of Athena, as the spirits of life in the
> light, and of life in the air, opposed each to their own contrary
> deity of death—Apollo to the Python, Athena to the Gorgon.
> (20:142)

Pater too closely associates Greek art and religion—"Out of Greek religion," Pater writes, "under happy conditions arises Greek art"
("Winckelmann," 43). For Pater, Greek religion is itself a magnificent
"poetical conception" of the titanic struggle between light and darkness, life and death. Echoing what Iser calls the dialectic of reconciliation, Pater asserts: "The Dorian cult of Apollo, rational, chastened,
debonair, with his unbroken daylight, always opposed to the sad
Chthonian divinities, is the aspiring element, by force and spring of
which Greek religion sublimes itself" (43). Not only do we see here
the harmonizing of oppositions in Pater's syncretism; we also find a
not so veiled reference to the primitive Greek religion, elements of
which survive for Pater in Wordsworthian pastoral. For both Pater
and Ruskin, however, it is the presence of those "sad Chthonian divinities" that gives to Greek religion and art its power and glory.

   But now we reach a significant difference in the two critics' attitudes toward Greek art. For Ruskin, the Greek naturalistic school is a
model for ethical and social behavior. Looking "stoutly into this
world," Greek faith encourages a preoccupation with the conditions of

the here and now as opposed to "the faith which dwells on the future" (7:267). For Pater, the great value of the Greek absorption in the present lies not in its social function, but rather in its "readiness for being ... turned into an object for the senses" ("Winckelmann," 43). Unlike the art of the Christian Middle Age, which is always "hinting at an idea which [it] cannot adequately express" (43), the art of ancient Greece perfectly embodies thought in sensuous form.

Pater dramatically illustrates the point by comparing the *Venus of Melos* to Fra Angelico's *Coronation of the Virgin* (fig. 3). Pater deems Angelico's fresco "a characteristic work of the middle age" (163), for it typifies medieval Christianity's "high indifference to the outward," its "crushing of the sensuous" (48). Pater's readers would have remembered that an engraving of the fresco had served as the frontispiece for Alexis-François Rio's *The Poetry of Christian Art*, the translation of his 1836 *De la poésie chrétienne*. For Rio, Fra Angelico was the "prime example of the 'Christian artist'" (Hill, 430). As I have already pointed out, Rio was a favorite of Ruskin's, and at least until the early 1850s Ruskin shared the French critic's enthusiasm for Angelico. Throughout *Modern Painters II* Ruskin wildly praises Angelico's work as the perfect type of the pure religious ideal. It is no accident, then, that Pater turns to Angelico to highlight the inadequacies of Christian art.

Ruskin's attitude toward Angelico shifted dramatically from the mid-1840s to the publication of *Modern Painters V* (Dellamora, "Revaluation," 142–50). During his 1845 tour of Italy he spent six weeks in Florence and was profoundly affected by Angelico, spending long hours copying the San Marco frescoes or the "three *perfectly* preserved" pictures in the sacristy of Santa Maria Novella (Ruskin, *Letters 1845*, 96). In a letter of July 1845 to his father, he divides his "scale of painters" into four classes and places Angelico at the head of the first, the class of "Pure Religious art. The School of Love." Angelico, Ruskin rhapsodizes, "[f]orms a class by himself—he is not an *artist*, properly so called, but an inspired saint" (*Letters 1845*, 144). The groupings form the basis of the distinction in *Modern Painters III* between the Purist and the Naturalist ideals, but Ruskin had not yet discerned the

Fig. 3. Fra Angelico, *Coronation of the Virgin*, 1440–41, Museo di San Marco, Florence (courtesy Alinari/Art Resource, NY)

limitations in Angelico and Purism that accompany his revaluation of the Greeks. As we have seen, that revaluation culminates in *Modern Painters V* where he vigorously attacks Christian art in its refusal to confront death, social injustice, and the sufferings of the here and now.[10]

Ruskin never wrote about the San Marco *Coronation of the Virgin*, but his youthful descriptions of Angelico's painting provide an instructive comparison to Pater's handling of the fresco. One of

Ruskin's favorite works of Angelico is the famous *Linaiuoli Triptych,* otherwise known as the *Tabernacle of the Linenweavers* (fig. 4). *Modern Painters II* ends in ecstatic praise of the angel choirs that dance along the frame of the Triptych, "with the flames on their white foreheads waving brighter as they move, and the sparkles streaming from their purple wings like the glitter of many suns upon a sounding sea" (4:332). Ruskin believed Angelico unequaled in rendering the gesture and movement of spiritual creatures. "I saw *angels* dancing today," he wrote to his father upon seeing the Triptych for the first time, "and so I know how *they* do it" (*Letters 1845,* 101).

A year after *Modern Painters II,* Ruskin published another account of the *Linaiuoli Triptych* in his long review of Lord Lindsay's *Sketches of the History of Christian Art.* Here he focuses not on the angelic choir of the frame, but rather on the Virgin and child painted on the three panels of the predella. The image provides an even more powerful representation of divine presence. In the purity of his color, the abstract character of his decoration, the symmetry of his design, the repose of his figures, Angelico transfigures mother and child into "signs or habitations of Divinity" (4:315). They are no more the human creatures they seem to be.

> In all the treatment Fra Angelico maintains his assertion of the authority of abstract imagination, which, depriving his subject of all material or actual being, contemplates it as retaining qualities eternal only—adorned by incorporeal splendour. The eyes of the beholder are supernaturally unsealed: and to this miraculous vision whatever is of the earth vanishes, and all things are seen endowed with an harmonious glory—the garments falling with strange, visionary grace, glowing with indefinite gold—the walls of the chamber dazzling as of a heavenly city—the mortal forms themselves impressed with divine changelessness—no domesticity—no jest—no anxiety—no expectation—no variety of action or of thought. Love, all fulfilling, and various modes of power, are alone expressed. (12:236–37)

Fig. 4: Fra Angelico, *Linaiuoli Triptych*, 1433–35, Museo di San Marco, Florence
(courtesy Erich Lessing/Art Resource, NY)

The painting inspires the contemplation of divinity, Ruskin suggests, through symbols of ideal tranquillity that transcend change. The Virgin shows no "complacency or petty watchfulness of maternity" (12:237); she is a symbol of divine love, serene, immutable.[11]

In his description of *The Coronation of the Virgin*, Pater too stresses the divine changelessness of Angelico's figures.

> In some strange halo of a moon sit the Virgin and our Lord, clad in mystical white raiment, half shroud, half priestly linen. Our Lord, with rosy nimbus and the long pale hair, *tanquam lana alba et tanquam nix*, of the figure in the Apocalypse, sets, with slender finger tips, a crown of pearl on the head of his mother, who, corpse-like in her refinement, bends to receive it, the light lying like snow upon her forehead. ("Winckelmann," 43)

To Pater's mind, Angelico's representation of divine presence brings, not a vision of harmonious glory, but rather an almost Gothic-like vision of the Un-Dead, a corpse-like Virgin half enclosed with her Son in a white shroud. The impression dissolves into a more conventional notion of purity associated with whiteness. In her refinement, Mary is free from impurities, clean and white and unchanging, like the pearls on her crown. Her Son's hair is pale—"white like wool, as white as snow." But in Pater's description there is a touch of irony, a sense of something cold and dead in the divine changelessness of the figures. Pater critiques precisely the "authority of abstract imagination" that Ruskin had praised in his comments on the *Linaiuoli Triptych*. The figures of Angelico's fresco "are at best overcharged symbols," Pater argues, "a means of hinting at an idea which art cannot adequately express, which still remains in the world of shadows" ("Winckelmann," 43). Ruskin remarks of Angelico, "whatever might merely please the eye, or interest the intellect, he despised, and refused" (12:241). Pater agrees, but describes it as an inadequacy. He "would have shrunk," Pater writes, "from the notion that what the eye apprehended was all" (43).

Far behind the religious mysticism of the Christian Middle Age stands the ideal art of the Greeks, represented for Pater in the *Venus of Melos* (fig. 5). As opposed to Angelico's fresco, the work of Greek art "is in no sense a symbol, a suggestion of anything beyond its own victorious fairness" ("Winckelmann," 43). Ruskin's well-known estimate of the statue was made in *The Queen of the Air*: "She has tranquil, regular, and lofty features; but could not hold her own for a moment against the beauty of a simple English girl, of pure race and kind heart" (19:413), implying, as he makes more explicit in an 1883 note to *Modern Painters II*, that "Greek idealism is dull." Ruskin never saw much ideal beauty in Greek art and he especially disliked the classic Greek countenance. What Ruskin valued was the Greeks' unflinching representation of truth (Keefe, 70). He stressed the Greek love of a "universal spottiness and chequeredness," the delight in "crossed or starred or spotted things" (20:350), the Greek conviction that human nature was a "barred and broken thing" (20:171).

In sharp contrast, Pater values the pure white light of Greek sculpture, "purged from the angry, blood-like stains of action and passion . . . opposed to man's restless movement" ("Winckelmann," 45). For Pater, the Hellenic ideal is characterized by "blitheness or repose" and "generality or breadth" (45), but above all by restraint. Pater recognizes that the Olympians do think beyond their own "victorious fairness," for he describes their placid minds as troubled with thoughts of decay and dispossession. But the ideal art of the Greeks is made possible by the renunciation of expression. Passion is kept "always below" that "degree of intensity" that causes the features to betray "anger, or desire, or surprise" (46). The Hellenic ideal, says Pater, "has nothing in common with the 'grotesque'" (46). In this way the Greek achieves an ideal art in which thought is saturate and identical with sensuous form. "The Greek mind had advanced to a particular state of self-reflection," Pater explains, "but was careful not to pass beyond it" (43). Quoting provocatively from Swinburne, the infamous poet of pagan worship, Pater praises Greek respect for the "'lordship of the soul'":

Fig. 5. *The Venus of Melos*, Louvre, Paris (courtesy Alinari/Art Resource, NY)

that lordship gives authority and divinity to human eyes and
hands and feet; nature is thrown into the background. But there
Greek thought finds its happy limit; it has not yet become too
inward; the mind has not begun to boast of its independence of
the flesh; the spirit has not yet absorbed everything with its
emotions, nor reflected its own colour everywhere. (43)

The Greek ideal, then, in Pater's analysis, "expressed itself preeminently" in sculpture of the human form, specifically the young male
body. Greek sculpture "deals almost exclusively with youth" (46), Pater
writes. If he could save only one piece of Hellenic art from the ravages
of time he thinks it might be that line of youths on the Panathenaic
frieze, "with their level glances, their proud patient lips, their chastened reins, their whole bodies in exquisite service" (46). As Richard
Jenkyns observes, the suppressed excitement of the description is easy
to hear, as it is in so many passages of the Winckelmann essay
(Jenkyns, 151). Winckelmann himself, in Pater's description, proves
his affinity with Hellenism and the spirit of Greek sculpture "by his
romantic, fervid friendships with young men" ("Winckelmann," 40).

We might say that in his celebration of the Greek ideal and its
white light, centrality, blitheness and repose, Pater is less of a revisionist than Ruskin, who insists on the Greek encounter with sorrow and
death and who has little interest in the Greek ideal of beauty. But
Pater's revisionary Hellenic ideal is of another kind. While he recognizes the "sad Chthonian divinities" of Greek religion, his aim, at least
in the Winckelmann essay, is to legitimate or justify masculine love by
associating it with the Greek ideal and its purity, spirituality, serenity,
and impressive restraint. As Greek sculpture derives from a kind of
sublimation or control of the passions, so Winckelmann is "free" from
the "kind of intoxication" that threatens the artist in his embrace of the
sensual world: "he fingers those pagan marbles with unsinged hands,
with no sense of shame or loss" (47).

By the 1850s and 1860s Greek studies at Oxford, and Victorian
Hellenism in general, were identified with political liberalism and

university reform (Dowling, *Hellenism and Homosexuality*; Turner; Jenkyns). Liberal partisans such as Benjamin Jowett, Matthew Arnold, W. E. Gladstone, and John Stuart Mill deployed Hellenism as a "discursive language of sociocultural renewal" (Dowling, *Hellenism and Homosexuality*, 35) in opposition to the stifling uniformity of industrialism and narrow religious fundamentalism. When Pater wrote "Winckelmann" in 1867, therefore, he was able to exploit and extend an already established liberal discourse of Victorian Hellenism. As Linda Dowling has demonstrated, along with Symonds, Wilde, and other Uranian poets, Pater radicalized the assumptions of Victorian liberal Hellenism by developing a coded version of liberalism, a homosexual counterdiscourse justifying male love.

While the counterdiscourse of the Oxford Hellenists may have been "coded" or hidden, it was no secret to Ruskin. On more than one occasion in his Oxford lectures Ruskin expressed serious reservations about Greek culture, especially the preoccupation with the physical beauty of the male body, which "arrested the ethical . . . progress of the Greek mind" (20:91). It is reasonable to read these public statements of disapproval in the context of the Oxford Hellenists. "Scarcely any of the moral power of Greece depended upon her admiration of beauty, or strength in the body," Ruskin argued in an 1872 lecture. "The mere admiration of physical beauty in the body, and the arts which sought its expression, not only conduced greatly to the fall of Greece, but were the cause of errors and crimes in her greatest time which must for ever sadden our happiest thoughts of her, and have rendered her example almost useless to the future" (22:235–36). But this is Ruskin at his most hyperbolic. The lectures of the 1870s demonstrate again and again the enormous aesthetic and spiritual influence Ruskin attributes to the Greeks. Indeed, Ruskin's intensive study of the Greeks ultimately leads to his "reconversion" to purist Christian art.[12]

Pater's conception of the Greek ideal owes much to Hegel's notion of the ideal in art and its concomitant appeal to the senses. This debt is more easily recognized in the original 1867 essay than in the revised version included in subsequent editions of *The Renaissance.*[13]

> Under what conditions does Greek religion thus transform itself into an artistic ideal? "Ideal" is one of those terms which through a pretended culture have become tarnished and edgeless. How great, then, is the charm when in Hegel's writings we find it attached to a fresh, clear-cut conception! With him the ideal is a *Versinnlichen* of the idea—the idea turned into an object of sense. ("Winckelmann," 43)

Ruskin had also complained that the term "ideal" had become too feeble in its modern usage, and in *Modern Painters III* he set out to clarify and improve the modern understanding of the word (Hill, 442). Pater's adoption of Hegel, however, and his concept of the "ideal" as "the idea turned into an object of sense" deliberately avoids Ruskin's praise of the mimetic:

> By the idea, stripped of its technical phraseology, he [Hegel] means man's knowledge about himself and his relation to the world, in its most rectified and concentrated form. This, then, is what we have to ask about a work of art—Did it at the age in which it was produced express in terms of sense, did it present to the eye or ear, man's knowledge about himself and his relation to the world in its most rectified and concentrated form? ("Winckelmann," 43)

This passage is consistent with Pater's elevation of Wordsworth as a modern ideal and, using Hegel, bolsters his tacit argument with Ruskin over the place of concentrated self-reflection as an ideal of artistic production.

Pater also uses Hegel against Ruskin in distinguishing the formal properties of the various arts and denoting the form of art which, according to the "limitations of its material," most adequately expresses the various types of human temperament (Hill, 432; Inman, *Pater's Reading*, 132–33). Following Hegel, Pater maintains that the complexity of modern life is best expressed in painting, music, and poetry. These are the quintessential romantic arts, most capable of conveying the intricacies of human thought and character, the preoccupations of self-consciousness that mark this late stage in the development of the human mind. In contrast, architecture, "which begins in a practical need," is the form least expressive of both the human form and human mind.

> As human form is not the subject with which it deals: architecture is the mode in which the artistic effort centres when the thoughts of man concerning himself are still indistinct, when he is still little preoccupied with those harmonies, storms, victories of the unseen intellectual world, which wrought out into the bodily form, give it an interest and significance communicable to it alone. ("Winckelmann," 44)

For Pater (and Hegel), architecture is the art least capable of confronting the modern condition, least "incidental to a consciousness brooding with delight over itself" (45). Ruskin's intricate analysis of Venetian architecture as reflecting the history of the city's ethical life is inadequate, for the medium itself is incapable of expressing the complexity of modern ethical concerns, the first expressions of which belong to the Renaissance. For Pater, architecture is a more appropriate reflection of ancient Egypt, an even earlier stage than Greece in the development of the human mind, "according to Hegel's beautiful comparison, a Memnon waiting for the day, the day of the Greek spirit, the humanistic spirit, with its power of speech" (44).

Winckelmann, ever perfecting his "reconciliation to the spirit of Greek sculpture," is ultimately subject to its same limitations. Unable to penetrate into the darkness and chaos of Aeschylean tragedy and Greek mythology, Winckelmann "could hardly have conceived of the subtle and penetrative, but somewhat grotesque art of the modern world" (47). As the type of the modern artistic temperament, Pater turns to Winckelmann's successor, Goethe, who successfully fuses the romantic temper with the classical. Sounding the notes of revolt and antinomianism and strangeness that Pater always associates with the romantic, Goethe simultaneously preserves the supreme characteristics of the Hellenic ideal.[14]

> Goethe illustrates that union of the Romantic, its adventure, its variety, its deep subjectivity, with Hellenism, its transparency, its rationality, its desire of beauty—that marriage of Faust and Helena, of which the art of the nineteenth century is the child, the beautiful lad Euphorion, as Goethe conceives him, on the crags in the "splendour of battle," "in harness as for victory," his brows bound with light. (49)

In Goethe, Pater discovers a solution to what he describes as a central problem of modern culture: amidst the "conflicting claims," "entangled interests," many sorrows and preoccupations of the modern world, "the problem of unity with ourselves in blitheness and repose, is far harder than it was for the Greek within the simple terms of antique life" (49). Faced with the unsettling discoveries of contemporary science and philosophy, "[c]an we bring down that ideal into the gaudy, perplexed light of modern life?" (49).

Pater expresses Goethe's solution in a memorable phrase from the "Conclusion," "that strange, perpetual weaving and unweaving of ourselves." Completeness and serenity in modern life is achieved only through a refusal to acquiesce in any orthodoxy, opinion, theory, point of view. Only a life of perpetual renunciations can free one, or give the sense of being free, from the entangling distractions and bewilderments of modernity. What is meant by Goethe's description, "life in the whole—*im Ganzen?*" Pater asks. "It means the life of one for whom, over and over again, what was once precious has become indifferent" (49). "With a kind of passionate coldness such natures rejoice to be away from and past their former selves" (49). Pater's oxymoron reflects the difficult union of romantic and classical that characterizes the "supreme, artistic view" of modern life. The romantic passion and strangeness of modernity are met by the modern artist, or he who aims at a life of artistic perfection, with the cold repose and rationality of the antique ideal.

Like Pater's Wordsworth, who is the poet of nature because he is capable of aestheticizing nature, Goethe gives form to his "large vision"; his "culture did not remain 'behind the veil': it ever abutted on the practical functions of art" (50). Along with the romances of Victor Hugo, a modern writer for whom Ruskin feels enormous disdain, Goethe's romances represent, for Pater, "high examples of modern art dealing thus with modern life; it regards that life as the modern mind must regard it, but reflects upon it blitheness and repose" (50).

Pater's history of temperament—from the Greek through the medieval and into the modern—is characterized by continuity, recurrence, and an interplay between the classical and romantic tempers. This interplay culminates in the modern art of Goethe and Hugo but it is already evident in Hellenic culture. Winckelmann himself, in Pater's characterization, embodies the survival of the Greek temperament. Unlike the modern, many-sided Goethe, Winckelmann's perfection is a narrow one. He exclusively pursues the "central enthusiasm" of his life, the observation of Greek life, the interpretation of the Hellenic spirit. In his integrity, in his "desperate faithfulness" to the one motive within him that is "native and strong," Winckelmann is a guide to the higher life, "to the life of the spirit and the intellect." "One learns nothing from him," Goethe says of Winckelmann, "but one becomes something" (quoted in "Winckelmann," 38). This ethic, as we have seen, is echoed in the explicit dogma of the Wordsworth essay. " That the end of life is not action, but contemplation—*being* as distinct from *doing*— a certain disposition of the mind: is, in some shape or other, the principle of all the higher morality" ("Wordsworth," 465).

Devoted to a life of impassioned contemplation, the ideal recep-
tive spectator possesses a complementary instinct toward the sensual,
the impulse, as Pater writes of Winckelmann, "to escape from abstract
theory to intuition, to the exercise of sight and touch" ("Winckelmann," 38). Winckelmann's passionate, romantic friendships with
young men perfect "his reconciliation to the spirit of Greek sculpture"
(40). He betrays his temperament even in appearance, "by the olive
complexion, his deep-seated, piercing eyes, the rapid movements"
(40). He somehow apprehends "the subtlest principles of the Hellenic
manner" through a mere touch, catching "the thread of a whole se-
quence of laws in some hollowing of the hand, or dividing of the hair"
(40). To Pater, he seems to manifest the old heresy of Origen, the
fancy of the Platonists:

> he seems to realize that fancy of the reminiscence of a forgotten
> knowledge hidden for a time in the mind itself, as if the mind of
> one, [lover and philosopher at once in some phase of preexis-
> tence] fallen into a new cycle, were beginning its intellectual ca-
> reer over again, yet with a certain power of anticipating its
> results. (40)[15]

In the Wordsworth essay, as we have seen, Pater identifies the "Intimations" ode as the poet's crucial expression of palingenesis. Unlike
Wordsworth, however, Winckelmann cannot engage in the imaginative recollection of childhood as the source of his ideal past. The
memories of Winckelmann's youth bring feelings of dejection rather
than compensation, an effective de-idealization of the Wordsworthian
child of nature.

> The child of a poor tradesman, he enacted in early youth an ob-
> scure struggle, the memory of which ever remained in him as a
> fitful cause of dejection. In 1763, in the full emancipation of his
> spirit, looking over the beautiful Roman prospect, he writes,
> "One gets spoiled here; but God owed me this; in my youth I
> suffered too much." (37)

According to Pater's somewhat quirky psychology, Winckelmann turns in place of his own childhood to the Greek spirit, the "unperplexed youth of humanity," for his vision of an ideal past. The recovery of that past is his means toward the cultivation of a higher life.

> To him, closely limited except on the side of the ideal, building for his dark poverty a house not made with hands, it early came to seem more real than the present. In the fantastic plans of travel continually passing through his mind, to Egypt, for instance, and France, there seems always to be rather a wistful sense of something lost to be regained, than the desire of discovering anything new. (37)

The typical Paterian metaphor of the house as mind (Meisel, *Absent Father*, 123–25)—"The airy building of the brain," as Pater writes in "Wordsworth"—connects Winckelmann with both Wordsworth and Florian Deleal. Winckelmann's house not made with hands is his reconstruction of the cultural unity of Greece, as Florian's "house of thoughts" is his reconstruction of the house of his childhood. Pater's narrative of the return to a mythical-historical Eden, however, does not end in the Wordsworthian compensatory perception of "types and symbols of Eternity." The mouldering of flesh and bones is both inevitable and foreseen.

> It is with a rush of home-sickness that the thought of death presents itself. He would remain at home for ever on the earth if he could; as it loses its colour, and the senses fail, he clings ever closer to it; but since the mouldering of bones and flesh must go on to the end, he is careful for charms and talismans that may chance to have some friendly power in them when the inevitable shipwreck comes. ("Winckelmann," 42)

The return through imagination, whether to an idealized childhood or to a historical age, effects no transcendent escape from material existence. Pagan worship, Pater suggests, like Christian consolation, owes its existence to this "universal pagan sentiment," which "measures the sadness with which the human mind is filled" (42). The cultivation of charms and talismans is "the eternal stock of all religions," the "anodyne which the religious principle, like one administering opiates to the incurable, has added to the law which makes life sombre for the vast majority of mankind" (42). Such a tragic romance, demanding the ritualistic annihilation of the natural, and offering for that sacrifice such ephemeral rewards, is a view of life Ruskin steadily rejects.

Three 🖙 Leonardo, Michelangelo, and the Oxford Lectures

O THER than "Winckelmann," first published in 1867, Pater composed each of the essays for *Studies in the History of the Renaissance* during Ruskin's first tenure at Oxford as Slade Professor of Fine Art. From 1869 to 1873, Pater devoted himself to criticism of the visual arts, publishing articles on Leonardo, Botticelli, and Michelangelo, reviewing Sidney Colvin's book on Italian and English design, and finishing *Studies in the History of the Renaissance*. Pater's essay on Michelangelo follows Ruskin's Oxford lecture on the artist by only five months, and his sympathy is in stark contrast to Ruskin's ferocious condemnation of the Renaissance giant. Pater's "Notes on Leonardo da Vinci," his first signed article, was published in 1869, Ruskin's first year as Slade Professor. In contrast to the almost evangelical tone of the inaugural lectures, Pater's essay offered a more sensuous and remote appreciation of the fine arts, a distinctly more modern voice than the voluble Slade Professor.

The Slade Professor

Ruskin believed deeply that his lectures to a university audience were among his most important work. In a conversation with the art critic M. H. Spielmann, he insisted that "I have taken more pains with the Oxford Lectures than with anything else I have ever done, and I must say that I am immensely disappointed at their not being more constantly quoted and read. What have I ever done better than this?" (20:xxii). His early drafts of the first Oxford Lectures reveal an enormous amount of rewriting, both in the revision of language and the rearranging of the order of his topics. "I believe that I am taking too much trouble in writing these lectures," Ruskin writes in a note to *Ariadne Florentina*. "This sentence has cost me, I suppose, first and last, about as many hours as there are lines in it" (20:xlviii). Yet audiences were enormous, and in describing the success of his first couple of talks Ruskin wrote to his mother, "I really think the time has come for me to be of some use."[1]

To Ruskin's disappointment, many of his plans and dreams for the Slade Professorship, as outlined in his inaugural lecture, did not come to fruition. In his preface to the 1887 edition of the *Lectures on Art*, Ruskin acknowledges that the "sanguine utterances" of the first few lectures "have remained unfulfilled." The drawing school attracted few serious students—on the average only two or three undergraduates would attend lessons—and the proposed schools of sculpture, architecture, metal work, and manuscript illumination were never established. Because no specified examinations were given in the fine arts, Ruskin's ambitious plans were probably doomed from the beginning. His own "scattered" energies, as Ruskin points out, also helped to lessen his effectiveness. During the time of his two tenures, as Kenneth Clark remarks, Ruskin "published works on botany, geology, and ornithology; wrote guide books to Florence, Venice, Padua, and Amiens; arranged a collection for the study of art in the University galleries; founded a museum in Sheffield; organized the Guild of St. George" (*Ruskin at Oxford*, 5); and wrote, at monthly intervals, his letters to the workmen of Great Britain, *Fors Clavigera*. In addition, Ruskin's commitment to addressing the social problems faced by the English working class was often perceived as being at odds with his role and function as professor of fine art. His audience at Oxford was, of course, very different from the working-class readers he addressed in his social criticism and political economy—the intended audience of *Time and Tide* and *Fors* (Austin, 20–43). This apparent dichotomy of interest and audience aroused some suspicion in Oxford, and his efforts to form St. George's Guild "made all my Oxford colleagues distrustful of me, and many of my Oxford hearers contemptuous" (20:13).

Nonetheless, the lectures were an event, and they attracted masses of undergraduates, as well as all of Oxford's most distinguished personages. Henry Nevinson remembers the lectures as having made the "deepest impression" on him, "the depth of thought and the passion of indignation . . . raised his lectures far above the religious height of the most solemn services I have heard" (54). And Collingwood recalls Ruskin's manner of delivery, the first half hour most often occupied in a careful and mannered reading of his prepared notes until suddenly,

> he would break off, and with quite another air extemporise the liveliest interpolations, describing his diagrams or specimens, restating his arguments, re-enforcing his appeal. His voice, till then artificially cadenced, suddenly became vivacious; his gestures, at first constrained, became dramatic. He used to act his subject, apparently without premeditated art, in the liveliest pantomime. (272)

The published lectures do not, of course, contain the asides and moments of spontaneity that must have contributed much to Ruskin's appeal. Cook and Wedderburn describe Ruskin as having a "smile that was never long absent when he lectured," and they recall his delight at having held up a sketch of Tintoretto's *Paradise* upside down. "'Ah, well,' he said, joining in the general laughter, 'what does it matter? for in Tintoret's 'Paradise' you have heaven all round you" (20:xxvi–xxvii).

Ruskin's *Lectures on Art* are surely some of his most forceful and didactic pronouncements on art and life. In order to address the undergraduates at Oxford he adopts a sermonizing tone, and the titles of the first few lectures even manifest the Latin root of the word sermon, *serere*—to link together:"The Relation of Art to Religion," "The Relation of Art to Morals," "The Relation of Art to Use." This is what Ruskin wants most to impress upon his young audience—"the grave relations of human art . . . to human life" (20:95–96). In his inaugural lecture he spells out his purpose very plainly:"Now listen to me . . . for this is what I have chiefly to say to you. The art of any country *is the exponent of its social and political virtues*" (20:39). This was, of course, the message of *The Stones of Venice*, almost twenty years earlier. The story of the rise and fall of Venice is both reflected in and reflected by the history of the city's architecture and architectural ornament. But the warning uttered to Victorian England by "the fast-gaining waves, that beat like passing bells" against Venice, is now sounded even more urgently and more directly. Ruskin no longer confronts England's social and cultural crisis through the mirror of history. He is preaching directly to English youth, and he is explicitly concerned with the "present state of the practice of the arts in England" (20:22) and therefore, necessarily, with the present state of the social, political, and ethical conditions of the country.

In his inaugural lecture, Ruskin paints a bleak picture of the condition of the arts in England. The rapid development of the system of commerce, the improved means of communication with foreign countries, the sudden creation of a vast and uninformed patronage, and the increasing demand for popular art are all detrimental to the creation of vital and excellent art, and instead encourage mediocrity and mass production.[2] Ruskin's purpose and burden as professor of fine art is to convince his audience of the cultural crisis he describes, and to provide them with the guidance and resolve to combat such a crisis. He believes it the function of his Professorship

> to establish both a practical and critical school of fine art for English gentlemen: practical, so that, if they draw at all, they may draw rightly; and critical, so that, being first directed to such works of existing art as will best reward their study, they

> may afterwards make their patronage of living artists delightful
> to themselves in their consciousness of its justice, and, to the ut-
> most, beneficial to their country, by being given to the men who
> deserve it; in the early period of their lives, when they both need
> it most and can be influenced by it to the best advantage.
> (20:27–28)

Ruskin is explicitly concerned with the education of future patrons.
He must work to fashion their critical faculties so that the enjoyment
of art will come from the "consciousness of its justice," a consciousness
of the just and proper handling of its materials and subject. This is the
proper and necessary stance of the spectator of art, and it will result in
the support of only the most deserving artists. "You can have noble art
only from noble persons" (20:39), Ruskin cries. The great arts support
and exalt human life, but the great arts cannot exist if the social, political, and ethical state of that human life is not virtuous:

> we *may* have splendour of art again, and with that, we may truly
> praise and honour our Maker, and with that set forth the beauty
> and holiness of all that He has made: but only after we have
> striven with our whole hearts first to sanctify the temple of the
> body and spirit of every child that has no roof to cover its head
> from the cold, and no walls to guard its soul from corruption, in
> this our English land. (20:71)

This is an example of Ruskin's belief in continuity, which I noted in
the introduction; it is also emblematic of his despair regarding the rebirth of the Gothic spirit in his own time.

Ruskin is preaching conversion, and he must persuade his young
listeners of the gravity of his and their task. As the lectures continue,
his rhetoric becomes more and more urgent and impassioned. In his
second series of lectures, *Aratra Pentelici*, he compares the sculpture of
modern England to that of ancient Greece as "literally one of corrupt
and dishonourable death, as opposed to bright and fameful life"

(20:240). "And now," Ruskin asks, "will you bear with me while I tell you finally why this is so?"

> The cause with which you are personally concerned is your own frivolity; though essentially this is not your fault, but that of the system of your early training. But the fact remains the same, that here, in Oxford, you, a chosen body of English youth, in nowise care for the history of your country, for its present dangers, or its present duties. You still, like children of seven or eight years old, are interested only in bats, balls, and oars. (20:240)

He will echo this complaint against his students' frivolity throughout his tenure as Slade Professor. The famous road-building scheme at Ferry Hincksey, which began in the spring of 1874, was his most dramatic attempt to teach his students the rewards of work done in the service of others. Instead of wasting away hours learning "to leap and to row, to hit a ball with a bat," Ruskin wished his students to experience the "pleasures of *useful* muscular work, and especially of the various and amusing work involved in getting a Human Pathway rightly made through a lovely country, and rightly adorned" (20:xliii). He exhorted them to "d-i-g, dig, go and do it" (20:xlv). Ruskin's unaffected enthusiasm attracted great admiration, and it was primarily the force and brilliancy of his personality that drew so many young men, including Oscar Wilde, to rise before dawn and go dig a road. There was also the reward of the breakfast that Ruskin would host after each day's work. Wilde's first year at Oxford was 1874, and it was during the few months of road-building in the spring that Ruskin and Wilde began their friendship. Wilde, along with so many others, had attended Ruskin's lectures that term, "always leaning his large and flabby form against the door, conspicuous for something unusual in his dress" (Nevinson, 55).

G. W. Kitchin, in his short and anecdotal "Ruskin at Oxford," points out that the primary target of Ruskin's road-building scheme was the sporting culture at Oxford, which had grown more prevalent throughout the 1860s, but he also suggests that the road-building was directed against the phenomenon of aestheticism. "[I]t was also invented in order to weed out those feeble folk—the Postlethwaites and Maudles—who caricature the artistic man of genius, and try to make repartees, and are a compound of conceit and weakness" (45–46). As Tim Hilton demonstrates, however, Ruskin's diggings worked rather to encourage the emerging aestheticism, marking "the beginning of an opposition within English educational culture of aesthetic interests and the sporting ethos" (228). Ruskin's behavior and language undoubtedly contributed to the social style of aestheticism at Oxford (his habitual use of the phrase "entirely precious," for example). This style, however, as Hilton reminds us, had not yet developed. George Du Maurier would create Postlethwaite and Maudle only in 1880. But Kitchin clearly senses Ruskin's antipathy to the ideas that that social style will invoke—that art is self-sufficient and need serve no didactic purpose.

Leonardo

As the most distinguished English critic of the arts, Ruskin enjoyed the authority of the Slade Professorship. Pater's status was far less impressive. A university don and classical scholar who had received no professional training in the fine arts, Pater was neither an artist or draftsman (like Ruskin), nor a professional art critic. His writing, however, began to attract more and more attention at Oxford, culminating in the outrage and excitement provoked by the "Conclusion." Pater's celebration of an exotic and brooding Leonardo, touched with "the fascination of corruption," and "possessed of curious secrets and a hidden knowledge," was, especially to many of the undergraduates at Oxford, far more alluring than the dogmatic criticism of the older Ruskin.

The Leonardo essay marks the achievement of the Paterian style, and establishes a sharp contrast not only to the thunderous and prophetic style of much of Ruskin's writing, but also to Ruskin's characteristic critical method, in which works of art are utilized as polemical illustrations of some specific interpretation of history or culture. In the Leonardo essay, for the first time, Pater employs what becomes his distinctive critical method, in which the work of art is made to stand as a metonymical representation of the artist's special temperament, a method Pater most likely discovered in Swinburne (Bullen, "Historiography," 162–65). Pater might also have discovered in Swinburne the means by which the critic's verbal description of a visual image could be used to express the temperament of the critic himself. The title of Pater's article echoes Swinburne's 1868 "Notes on Designs of the Old Masters at Florence," and Pater explicitly credited Swinburne with having inspired his study.[3]

Swinburne's essay is a record of impressions and affective responses, rather than a close description of Tuscan designs. "I have aimed," writes Swinburne, "at nothing further than to cast into some legible form my impression of the designs registered in so rough and rapid a fashion" (15:156). Leonardo is the first of the more than thirty artists Swinburne considers, and his evocation of the "painter's chosen type of woman" stands behind Pater's Mona Lisa. By providing Pater with an explicit model in which the perceiving consciousness of the critic is the focus of the critical essay, Swinburne paved the way for the invention of Pater's aesthetic critic, given theoretical substance in the "Preface," but already anticipated in Pater's description of the ideal critical temperament, as represented by Winckelmann.

Pater's Leonardo exhibits many of the major Renaissance tendencies Ruskin had denounced in *The Stones of Venice*, including excessive pride, a lack of religious feeling, a strong spirit of mockery and jest, and an inexhaustible interest in science. The "painter who has fixed the outward type of Christ for succeeding centuries," writes Pater in the essay's first paragraph, "was a bold speculator, holding lightly by other men's beliefs, setting philosophy above Christianity" ("Notes on Leonardo," 494). Trifling with his genius, wasting many days in "curious tricks of design," his great works are crowded into "a few tormented years of later life" (494). To others he appears weary and dissatisfied—"his restlessness, his endless retouchings, his odd experiments with colour. How much must he leave unfinished, how much recommence!" (501). His "boundless curiosity" results in an intense and close analysis of the natural world, and he is found often in the company of men of science, his own scientific reflections filling thirteen volumes of manuscript. Penetrating so deeply into nature's secrets, Leonardo is drawn not only to the beautiful in nature, but also to her grotesques—"the *bizarre* or *recherché* in landscape" (500). "Legions of grotesques sweep under his hand" (497). In his art, Leonardo combines the extremes of beauty and terror, creating images of a strange sublimity. "But mingled inextricably with this," observes Pater, "there is an element of mockery also; so that, whether in sorrow or scorn, he caricatures Dante even" (497).

In June 1869, the probable time of the composition of Pater's essay and five months before its publication (Inman, *Pater's Reading*, 201), Ruskin published *The Queen of the Air*, in which was included his most provocative and disparaging comments on Leonardo. Pater could have read these comments as early as July 1865 when Ruskin originally published them as part of an article in the *Art Journal*. Ruskin unfavorably compares Leonardo to the painter's student Luini, and emphasizes the Renaissance tendencies he had condemned in *Stones* and which he finds embodied in Leonardo.

> Because Leonardo made models of machines, dug canals, built fortifications, and dissipated half his art-power in capricious ingenuities, we have many anecdotes of him;—but no picture of importance on canvas, and only a few withered stains of one upon a wall. But because his pupil, or reputed pupil, Luini, laboured in constant and successful simplicity, we have no anecdotes of him;—only hundreds of noble works. (19:129–30)[4]

Ruskin's hyperbolic praise of Luini seems to the twentieth-century ear utterly perverse:

> [Luini] is a man ten times greater than Leonardo—a mighty colourist, while Leonardo was only a fine draughtsman in black,

staining the chiaroscuro drawing, like a coloured print: he perceived and rendered the delicatest types of human beauty that
have been painted since the days of the Greeks, while Leonardo
depraved his finer instincts by caricature, and remained to the
end of his days the slave of an archaic smile: and he is a designer
as frank, instinctive, and exhaustless as Tintoret, while Leonardo's
design is only an agony of science, admired chiefly because it
is painful, and capable of analysis in its best accomplishment.
(19:130)

Ruskin's censure of Leonardo's lack of sustained artistic effort is consistent with prevailing eighteenth- and nineteenth-century attitudes
toward the Renaissance artist, as expressed by Henry Fuseli or
Matthew Pilkington, for example (Bullen, "Walter Pater's 'Renaissance,'" 269–70).

Pater deviates from his English counterparts, finding in
Leonardo's capriciousness evidence of the artist's "boundless curiosity"
and quest for perfection, the chief elements of his genius. Inspired by
Michelet, Quinet, and especially Gautier, Pater, unlike Ruskin, revels
in the psychological intensity of the paintings, projections of
Leonardo's complex mental life. The anecdotes we have of the artist,
what Pater calls, after the French, his *legend*, is a great part of what
makes Leonardo so fascinating, "one of the most brilliant in Vasari"
("Notes on Leonardo," 494); Pater employs this legend dramatically to
"support" his analysis of the impressions made on him by Leonardo's
art. Like Ruskin, Pater seizes upon Leonardo's instinct toward the
grotesque—"he caricatures Dante even." Unlike Ruskin, however,
Pater exalts rather than condemns the irreverent and bizarre features
of Leonardo's work. Rather than a depravation of his finer instincts,
Leonardo's irreverence is an indispensable element of his genius,
"mingled inextricably" with his instinct toward the sublime.

Both critics note Leonardo's obsession with "the smiling of
women," culminating in the *Mona Lisa* (fig. 6). To Ruskin, that obses-

sion disfigures the painter's portraiture; he is not the master of his art, but the "slave," bound to an "archaic" smile from which Ruskin shrinks. Pater too apprehends the ancientness of that smile; she "is older than the rocks among which she sits" ("Notes on Leonardo," 507). But for Pater the Mona Lisa is not merely antiquated and grotesque, for she is at the same time always and eternally new, giving expression to the

Fig. 6. Leonardo da Vinci, *Mona Lisa*, 1503, Louvre, Paris (courtesy Alinari/Art Resource, NY)

"fancy of a perpetual life" and standing as "the symbol of the modern idea" (507). As Pater's Goethe represents unity with one's self, the Mona Lisa represents unity of being. She reconciles and sums up within herself all "modes of thought and life" (507).

Mysterious, expressive, eternal, archaic—Leonardo's *Mona Lisa* is Pater's quintessential artistic expression of the Renaissance spirit of unity. Dark and feminine, she stands in stark contrast to the bright and definite forms of classical beauty: "Set her for a moment beside one of those white Greek goddesses or beautiful women of antiquity, and how would they be troubled by this beauty, into which the soul with all its maladies has passed?" (506). As Pater had stated in "Winckelmann," sculpture is the art most suited for the sensuous expression of the Greek ideal, while poetry, music, and painting are the arts most capable of conveying the intricacies of the romantic spirit. The painting of *La Gioconda* conveys a beauty "wrought out from within upon the flesh—the deposit, little cell by cell, of strange thoughts and fantastic reveries and exquisite passions" (506). As an expression of romantic inwardness, the *Mona Lisa* is, following the history of artistic temperament laid out in "Winckelmann," an essentially modern work.[5] Pater's Mona Lisa exhibits strange, enigmatic qualities, qualities Pater explicitly associates with romanticism in his 1876 essay of that title. Her thoughts are "strange," and her eyelids a "little weary." Her smile is "sinister"; "like the vampire, she has been dead many times, and learned the secrets of the grave" (507). Her beauty embraces all the "maladies" of the soul.

The *Mona Lisa* stands as yet another of Pater's illustrations of the "fancy of a perpetual life," which he describes in "Wordsworth" as a permanent tendency of human thought. Pater even suggests that the picture is created out of time. "[W]as it in four years," he asks, "or in four months, and as by stroke of magic, that the image was projected?" (506). In contrast to Winckelmann, in whom the mechanism of metempsychosis is manifest only in a limited way—that is, in his focus on the Greek artistic ideal—the *Mona Lisa* embodies the function itself of metempsychosis. She represents for Pater a comprehensive vessel of recollected human experience.

Not only is the *Mona Lisa* Leonardo's masterpiece, but also, as a compendious icon "sweeping together ten thousand experiences," she is a mirror image of the modern philosopher's description of the human mind. As a metonymical representation of the artist's temperament, the *Mona Lisa* illustrates the modern qualities possessed by Leonardo himself. Pater, in fact, sees Leonardo as a link to the landscape instinct that comprises the survival of the romantic spirit in Pater's own day.

In his "return to nature," Pater's Leonardo anticipates Wordsworth. Just as Pater's Wordsworth possesses an "intimate consciousness of the expression of natural things," so Leonardo feels the "power of an intimate presence in the things he handled" (496). Beginning with the *Renaissance* edition of 1888, Pater turns to Bacon's phrase, "Homo minister et interpres naturae," that man is the minister and interpreter of nature, for the subtitle of the Leonardo essay.[6] Leonardo translates all the strange voices and expressions that bind people to the earth. He shares with Wordsworth the visionary strength to transfigure experience, given expression in the "pathetic power" of his painting and drawing.[7] In that moment of "*bien-être*," the moment of heightened vision, "the idea is stricken into colour and imagery" (501). Leonardo's strange and bizarre landscapes are the exceptional fruits of authentic spots of time: "Through his strange veil of sight things reach him so; in no ordinary night or day, but as in faint light of eclipse, or in some brief interval of falling rain at daybreak, or through deep water" (500). Leonardo's hermetic, mythopoetic art stands, for Pater, as the Renaissance's ideal expression of the romantic spirit. The natural world, filtered through the artist's mind, results in an exquisite expression of the "world within," granting us an elevating, even soothing influence, a sense "of the subtler forces of nature, and the modes of their action, all that is magnetic in it . . . where only the finer nerve and the keener touch can follow" (502).

As early as *Modern Painters I*, Ruskin had been critical of
Leonardo, and especially of his landscapes, which Ruskin described as
having had "an unfortunate effect on art" (3:183). Ruskin's 1849 trip to
the Louvre reaffirmed that impression. In his notes from that visit,
Ruskin groups the *Mona Lisa* with the *Virgin of the Rocks* and *St. Anne*
as expressions of Leonardo's landscape ideal, which he describes as artificial and grotesque. "What kind of mind could lead Leonardo to
adopt such an ideal?" notes Ruskin.

> Those blue icebergs appear to be his universal distance. In the
> St. Anne they rise out of a kind of sea, or wide river, with a weir
> upon it—these men who never drew landscape from nature
> *could* not get on without weirs—and form a cloudy, unfinished
> distance far away behind the heads, like an old map, some ideal
> of snow in extreme distance. . . . Behind the head of Mona Lisa,
> same thing, equally grotesque, blue and unfinished. (12:460)

Ruskin is responding to the very transfiguration of nature Pater
deems the strength of Leonardo's art.

Ruskin's attitude toward Leonardo, as well as toward other Renaissance masters like Raphael and Michelangelo, was actually far
more ambivalent than these comments might suggest and resembles
his attitude toward the modern English romantic poets Wordsworth
and Shelley. In *Stones*, Ruskin qualified his characterization of the Renaissance's "evil spirit" by claiming that the reader "will not find one
word but of the most profound reverence for those mighty men who
could wear the Renaissance armour of proof, and yet not feel it en-
cumber their living limbs. Leonardo and Michael Angelo, Ghirlan-
dajo and Masaccio, Titian and Tintoret" (11:18). By the time of the
Oxford lectures, as we will see, Ruskin had obviously come to believe
that Michelangelo's "armour of proof" had indeed smothered his vitality. But in his first series of lectures as Slade Professor Ruskin selected
as his textbook Leonardo's *Treatise on Painting*. This is in large part due
to the *Treatise's* endorsement of imitation in art. "What kind of representation of nature is best?" Ruskin asks his students.

> I will tell you in the words of Leonardo. "That is the most
> praiseworthy painting which has most conformity with the
> thing represented." . . . In plain terms, "the painting which is lik-
> est nature is the best." . . . Let the living thing, (he tells us,) be re-
> flected in a mirror, then put your picture beside the reflection,
> and match the one with the other. And indeed, the very best
> painting is unquestionably so like the mirrored truth, that all
> the world admits its excellence. (20:121)

In the *Treatise*, at least, Leonardo is an excellent model for Ruskin's
students.

Perhaps the grotesque blue icebergs represent evidence of
Leonardo's failure in practice, but in theory Ruskin seems to be in ac-
cordance. As so often in Ruskin, however, we find a contradiction even
on this subject. The Slade Professor also identifies Leonardo as a
"master" of the chiaroscuro school, the school of light and shade. As
such, he continually acknowledges the exceptional control and accuracy of Leonardo's drawing. He is the "most accomplished draughts-
man of Italy," used by Ruskin to teach his students the important
fundamentals of perspective (20:133).[8] He is "supreme in all questions
of execution" (20:158).

> You will often indeed see in Leonardo's work, and in Michael
> Angelo's, shadow wrought laboriously to an extreme of fineness;
> but when you look into it, you will find that they have always
> been drawing more and more form within the space, and never
> finishing for the sake of added texture, but of added fact.
> (20:158)

Leonardo's excellence in drawing shows itself in his close attention
to detail, an aspect of his work that had always greatly impressed
Ruskin. On returning from his 1854 summer tour, Ruskin again vis-
ited the Louvre, and was struck with the finish and attention to detail
in the St. Anne (fig. 7), characterizing that portion of the painting as
"Pre-Raphaelite" (12:473). He subsequently singles out the painting in

Fig. 7. Leonardo da Vinci, *Virgin and Child with St. Anne*, 1508–10, Louvre, Paris (courtesy Giraudon/Art Resource, NY)

his discussion of "finish" in art in *Modern Painters III*: "Thus tender in execution, and so complete in detail, that Leonardo must needs draw *every several vein in the little agates* and pebbles of the gravel under the feet of the St. Anne in the Louvre" (5:167).

Pater, too, singles out the St. Anne for its close attention to detail, finding in the "bright variegated stones, such as the agates in the *Saint Anne* . . . the apex of the older Florentine style of miniature painting, with patient putting of each leaf upon the trees and each flower in the grass" ("Notes on Leonardo," 496). And like Ruskin, Pater observes the intense "finish" of Leonardo's landscapes. Moving beyond that "old slight manner" of the Florentine style, Leonardo immerses himself in an ever more minute analysis of the natural world, developing a "microscopic sense of finish" derived from his observation of nature's "finesse, or delicacy of operation, that *subtilitas naturae* which Bacon notices" (499). It is the penetrative suggestion of life in nature, however, that is, for Pater, the great value of Leonardo's landscapes.

Michelangelo

"We must not fall into the paradox," warns John Addington Symonds in his *Life of Michelangelo Buonarroti*, "so perversely maintained by Ruskin in his lecture on Tintoretto and Michelangelo, that the latter was a cold and heartless artist, caring chiefly for the display of technical skill and anatomical science" (2:66). In Ruskin's lecture on Michelangelo, asserts Symonds, we see "how far a gifted writer can miss the mark through want of sympathy" (1:xix). When Symonds came to write his *Life*, published in 1892, he had access to the Buonarroti archives—which no one had ever had before. This collection of authentic contracts, letters, poems, and memoranda gave Symonds's *Life* an authority that previous biographies lacked and allowed him persuasively to counter Ruskin's depiction of the artist as hard and unfeeling. Symonds reveals a man possessed of strong feeling and tender emotion, a man much closer in temperament to that described by Pater, more than twenty years earlier, in his essay "The Poetry of

Michelangelo." "Mr. Pater," wrote Symonds in an 1873 review of that essay, "shows the truest sympathy for what has generally been over-looked in this stern master—his sweetness. The analysis of the nature of that sweetness is one of the triumphs of Mr. Pater's criticism."[9]

Although there is no direct evidence that Pater attended Ruskin's lecture, "The Relation between Michael Angelo and Tintoret," deliv-ered at Oxford on June 13, 1871, he must have been keenly interested in what Ruskin had to say. At a time when Pater was developing his own thoughts about the Renaissance artist, Ruskin's characterization of Michelangelo as "the chief captain of evil" of the Italian Renaissance provoked an enormous uproar throughout England's artistic and aca-demic community. The Slade Professor at London University, Ed-ward Poynter, expressed deep "indignation" and later delivered his own lecture in response, titled "Professor Ruskin on Michelangelo." Burne-Jones, after being treated by Ruskin to a private reading of the lecture, was so distressed that he threatened to drown himself in the Surrey Canal—"it didn't seem worth while to strive any more if he could think it and write it" (Burne-Jones, 2:18). Pater's essay appeared in the *Fortnightly Review* in November 1871, a mere five months after Ruskin's lecture. The timing does not appear to be coincidence.[10]

Pater's essay opens with a critical judgment, not directly of Michelangelo, but of his critics.

> Critics of Michelangelo have sometimes spoken as if the only characteristic of his genius were a wonderful strength, verging, as in the things of the imagination great strength al-ways does, on what is singular or strange. (559)

Ruskin is certainly one of those critics who highlight Michelangelo's great strength: he is "strong beyond all his companion workmen" (22:87). Where to many critics, however, this strength was to be praised, Ruskin deems Michelangelo's strength his great weakness; he is "never yet strong enough to command his temper or limit his aims"

(22:87; Bullen, "Pater and Ruskin," 59). Ruskin inherited from both the French and the English romantics the view that Michelangelo's strength was his chief value, but as J. B. Bullen points out, he "inverted the values that had become attached to it. Where French writers saw his power as the clearest evidence of his genius, Ruskin identified it with his decadence" ("Pater and Ruskin," 59).[11] Carried away by his own power, Michelangelo suffers from what to Ruskin is the artist's most crippling flaw—arrogance. Ruskin severely criticizes Michelangelo, as he had criticized Wordsworth, for excessive pride and vanity. Driven by an insatiable egotism, Michelangelo fails to fulfill—and, what is worse, precipitates a change in—what are to Ruskin "the four essentials of the greatest art":

1. Faultless and permanent workmanship.
2. Serenity in state or action.
3. The Face principal, not the body
4. And the Face free from either vice or pain. (22:85)

Michelangelo's agitated figures, frozen in moments of turmoil and motion, indicate his lower artistic value. Ruskin deems Michelangelo's preoccupation with strong and violently emotional incident a mere excuse for demonstrating his knowledge of human anatomy. In his attempt to "execute something beyond his power, coupled with a fevered desire that his power may be acknowledged" (22:87), Michelangelo sacrifices tranquillity for violence, the spirit of man for his flesh, bravado for instruction. "All that shadowing, storming, and coiling of his, when you look into it, is mere stage decoration, and that of a vulgar kind" (22:102).

Pater moves away from this critical fixation with Michelangelo's strength, calling attention to his sweetness and charm. Turning to Michelangelo's sonnets, especially those composed in later life, at the time of his Platonic intimacy with Vittoria Colonna, Pater discerns a reflective and dreamy attitude, free of stress and unruly emotion.

Their prevailing tone is a calm and meditative sweetness. The cry of distress is indeed there, but as a mere residue, a trace of bracing, chalybeate salt, just discernible in the song which rises as a clear sweet spring from a charmed space in his life. (565)

Pater acknowledges that a violent energy forms a great part of Michelangelo's temperament, but mingled with this strength is the constant effort to relax it. This effort is rewarded in the achievement of these temperate poems, composed during a period in Michelangelo's life "without which its excessive strength would have been so imperfect" (565).

By regarding Michelangelo as the culmination of fifteenth-century Tuscan sculpture, Pater is not merely dependent upon the sonnets to expose the tranquil and introspective side of the artist. Ruskin had portrayed Michelangelo as the instigator of the "deadly change," the mighty representative of the decadence associated with the Italian Counter-Reformation, polluting and exhausting the existing strengths of Italian art, the statesmanship and piety represented by the great Venetian master of the fifteenth century, John Bellini.[12] To Pater's Michelangelo, however, the melodramatic spirit of the Counter-Reformation is utterly alien. He had grown old and set in his ways, and the "world had changed around him" (566):

> Neo-catholicism had taken the place of the Renaissance. The spirit of the Roman Church had changed; . . . The opposition of the reform to art has been often enlarged on; far greater was that of the catholic revival. But in thus fixing itself in a frozen orthodoxy, the catholic church had passed beyond him, and he was a stranger to it. (566)

A stranger to the very artistic and spiritual developments of which Ruskin characterizes him the chief representative, Pater's Michelangelo looks only backwards. In his faith, he embodies the persistence of "that divine ideal" that hovers always "above the wear and tear of creeds" (567), and the religious controversies of the day. In his art, he resembles something like a Victorian imaginative anthropologist pursuing images of an elemental primitive culture.

> So he lingers on; a *revenant*, as the French say, a ghost out of another age, in a world too coarse to touch his faint sensibilities too closely; dreaming in a worn-out society, theatrical in life, theatrical in its art, theatrical even in its devotion, on the morning of the world's history, on the primitive form of man, on the images under which that primitive world had conceived of spiritual forces. (567)

Whereas Ruskin disparages Michelangelo's work as mere stage decoration, and that of a vulgar kind, Pater deliberately distinguishes the artist from the theatricality of his culture.

Pater's tracing of Michelangelo's heritage to the expressive sculpture of the fifteenth century is a relatively novel idea, made possible only by recent developments in the study of the period's sculpture.[13] Pater places Michelangelo securely in the tradition of the Florentine schools of the Middle Ages:

> if one is to distinguish the peculiar savour of his work, he must be approached, not through his followers, but through his predecessors; not through the marbles of Saint Peter's, but through the work of the sculptors of the fifteenth century over the tombs and altars of Tuscany. He is the last of the Florentines, of those on whom the peculiar sentiment of the Florence of Dante and Giotto descended. (567)

As the last of the Florentines, Michelangelo's art reflects the traditions of the medieval workman and preoccupations of the medieval mind. Like the medieval conceptions of *Tristram* or *Tannhäuser*, Michelangelo's conception of the *Creation of Man* is based on a conventional treatment of the subject. Sculpted "into a hundred carved ornaments of capital or doorway" (567), Michelangelo receives from this tradition "his central conception," and has but to "add the last touches in transferring it to the frescoes of the Sistine Chapel" (568).

While the medieval tradition of the Creation culminates in the Sistine Chapel, the sacristy of San Lorenzo stands as "the final expression" of the complementary tradition in fifteenth-century Florentine culture, the serious preoccupation with death. "*Outre-tombe!* *Outre-tombe!* is the burden of their thoughts," Pater writes, "from Dante to Savonarola" (568). Michelangelo devotes at least one half of his work to the adornment of tombs. But Pater calls special attention to the artist's persistent handling of a subject which was still in 1500 relatively new in Italian art, the *pietà*: "pity, the pity of the virgin mother over the dead body of Christ, expanded into the pity of all mothers over all dead sons, the entombment, with its cruel 'hard stones;' that is the subject of his predilection" (569). For Pater, the tenderness and "sentiment of profound pity" conveyed in the many forms of Michelangelo's *pietàs* complicate the prevailing image of the artist. It is his "professed disciples," Pater emphasizes, who are "in love with his strength only" (567) and never discern his sweetness and sadness. As I have already noted, Pater directly contradicts Ruskin by defending Michelangelo against the charge of theatricality, a quality Pater attributes only to the artist's followers. "Theatricality is their chief characteristic; and that is a quality as little attributable to Michelangelo, as to Mino or Luca Signorelli" (567). "They are always in dramatic attitudes," Ruskin complains of Michelangelo and Raphael, "and always appealing to the public for praise. They are the leading athletes in the gymnasium of the arts," concerned only with entertaining "the crowd of the circus" (22:88). "With him [Michelangelo]," Pater counters, "all is passionate, serious, impulsive" (567).

Pater begins to uncover the sweetness in Michelangelo, then, by noting the tone of his temperate poems and by locating him within the artistic tradition of the Florentine Middle Ages. But Pater discovers the real "secret of that sweetness" in the vitality of the sculpture, the surprising expression and play of life that Michelangelo achieves in his work with stone.

It belongs to the quality of his genius thus to concern itself almost exclusively with the creation of man. For him it is not, as in the story itself, the last and crowning act of a series of developments, but the first and unique act, the creation of life itself in its supreme form, off-hand and immediately, in the cold and lifeless stone. (560)

In effect, Pater's Michelangelo extends the fifteenth-century Florentine tradition of the Creation from a conventional subject of art to the very making of art itself. Unlike Leonardo, Pater tells us, Michelangelo possesses no instinctive sense of life or spirit in the natural world. He is no *interpres naturae*: "The world of natural things has almost no existence for him" (559). He traces no flowers like Leonardo, fills his backgrounds with no forest scenery like Titian's, "but only blank ranges of rock and dim vegetable forms as blank as they" (560). But in his sculptural creations of the human form, Pater senses a power "which brings into one's thoughts a swarm of birds and flowers and insects. The brooding spirit of life itself is there; and the summer may burst out in a moment" (561).

With this judgment Pater directly contradicts Ruskin, who explicitly condemns Michelangelo for sacrificing the spirit for the flesh. In contrast to the Greek or Venetian, Ruskin argues, Michelangelo's treatment of the body is "dishonest, insolent, and artificial" (22:98). In his desire to display mastery of the human anatomy, he relinquishes all expression of human spirit, creating lifeless figures of stone that reflect the corpses from which he gained his knowledge.

> Raphael and Michael Angelo learned it [the body] essentially from the corpse, and had no delight in it whatever, but great pride in showing that they knew all its mechanism; they therefore sacrifice its colours, and insist on its muscles, and surrender the breath and fire of it, for what is—not merely carnal,—but osseus, knowing that for one person who can recognize the loveliness of a look, or the purity of a colour, there are a hundred who can calculate the length of a bone. (22:97)

In sacrificing the human spirit, Ruskin contends, Michelangelo is incapable of creating figures that resemble human beings. His sculpture is invented for the purpose of demonstrating "ingenious mechanical motion" and of producing sensational effect. His excessive scientific knowledge mingled with extreme pride mar his genius and suffocate his spirit, extinguishing all life from his work.

> You are accustomed to think the figures of Michael Angelo sublime—because they are dark, and colossal, and involved, and mysterious,—because, in a word, *they look sometimes like shadows, and sometimes like mountains, and sometimes like spectres, but never like human beings.* Believe me, yet once more, in what I told you long since—man can invent nothing nobler than humanity. He cannot raise his form into anything better than God made it, by giving it *either the flight of birds or strength of beasts,* by enveloping it in mist, or heaping it into multitude. (22:101–2, my italics)

Ruskin accuses Michelangelo of a severe distortion of natural fact, but his offense is more grievous than the pathetic fallacy of Wordsworth or other "reflective" poets. Where Wordsworth habitually imparts to inanimate objects the feelings and emotions of a human being, thereby exhibiting and encouraging an excessive preoccupation with the self, Michelangelo transforms human beings into inanimate objects, the result of an egotism so excessive, a personality so vain, that it is unable to feel any sympathy whatsoever with human spirit. Unable to sympathize with human feeling, Michelangelo invests his figures with the severe outline or massive bulk of a mountain, the obscurity of a shadow, the incorporeality of a ghost. The art of Michelangelo, as described by Ruskin, is the inverse of the pathetic fallacy, creating death from life, the inanimate from the animate.

Pater seizes upon this objection, and in an ironic twist defends the artist against Ruskin's critique by presenting Michelangelo as a powerful exerciser of the pathetic fallacy. "[W]ith him," Pater writes of Michelangelo, "the very rocks seem to have life; they have but to cast away the dust and scurf to rise and stand on their feet" (560). His representations of nature are not imbued with human feeling and animation, indeed he gives us next to no representations of the natural world, but the very medium of his art *itself* is given life. He transforms the "cold and lifeless stone" into a seemingly animate, vital object.

> This creation of life, life coming always as relief or recovery, and always in strong contrast with the rough-hewn mass in which it is kindled, is in various ways the motive of all his work, whether its immediate subject be Pagan or Christian, legend or allegory; . . . Not the Judgment but the Resurrection is the real subject of his last work in the Sistine. (560)

In this passage, Pater emphasizes the relation of recovery to the creative impulse. The creation of art is an act of repossession, a recovery that brings with it relief and consolation. In drawing attention to the figure of the resurrection, Pater effects one of his reconciliations, allowing Michelangelo's technique to harmonize life and death: "With him the beginning of life has all the characteristics of resurrection; it is like the recovery of suspended health or animation, with its gratitude, its effusion, and eloquence" (560).

The notion of the beginning of life as resurrection is, of course, compatible with the doctrine of metempsychosis. Michelangelo's affinity with Neoplatonism and, as Pater says, its "vague and wistful" thoughts surrounding the "disembodied spirit," helps to form his profound understanding and expression of pity. Pater imagines in Michelangelo a predilection toward the unseen and unknown, rather than toward a fixed and definite conception of immortality. Although one might be hard pressed to find such a conception of immortality articulated in Ficino, it serves Pater well in his polarization of Dante and the Platonists:

> Dante's belief in immortality is formal, precise, and firm, as much so almost as that of a child who thinks the dead will hear,

if you cry loud enough. But in Michelangelo you have maturity, the mind of the grown man, dealing cautiously and dispassionately with serious things; and what hope he has is based on the consciousness of ignorance—ignorance of man, ignorance of the nature of the mind, its origin and capacities. (569)

Burdened by his paradoxical knowledge of ignorance, Michelangelo harbors no illusions as to the fate of the disembodied spirit, but heroically perseveres by giving life to stone uncovering traces of a prior state of existence and manifesting, at least in his art, a hope of recovery and palingenesis. For this reason, Michelangelo is yet another Paterian proof that the Renaissance of which the great artist is emblematic is an essentially romantic movement.

A year after publication of "The Poetry of Michelangelo," Pater wrote a brief essay on Luca della Robbia, most likely the last essay composed for *Studies in the History of the Renaissance.* Inman suggests that Pater originally intended to publish the essay as "Prelude to Michelangelo" *(Pater's Reading,* 315–17), and, as Kenneth Clark comments, "the admirable criticism of Michelangelo's sculpture as opposed to that of the Greeks . . . appears to be its only justification" ("Introduction," 18).[14] The distinctive limitation of sculpture, Pater explains, echoing and expanding upon his earlier comments in "Winckelmann," resides in the rigidity of its material, which encourages a tendency toward a "hard realism, a one-sided presentment of mere form" *(Renaissance,* 50–51). He is arguing that great schools of sculpture make an effort to overcome this limitation, to imbue their material with life and feeling; "each great system of sculpture resisting it in its own way, etherealising, spiritualising, relieving, its stiffness, its heaviness, and death" (51).

Michelangelo, Pater argues, overcomes this limitation by purposefully leaving his work in a state of incompletion. This solution, the finished figure never quite emerging from the stone, "suggests rather than realises actual form," and so achieves for his work an individual expression and spirit. "Well! that incompleteness is Michelangelo's equivalent for colour in sculpture; it is his way of etherealising pure form, of relieving its stiff realism, and communicating to it breath, pulsation, the effect of life" (*Renaissance*, 53). Michelangelo's incompleteness, Pater tells us, represents one of the three great styles of sculpture, each of which solved the problem of pure form in a different way.

In contrast to the system of Michelangelo stands the system of the Greek sculptors and their broad and universal treatment of humanity, what Winckelmann first described as *Allgemeinheit*. Classical sculpture is characterized by abstraction, the elimination of all that is particular to the individual in order to express the general type, thus representing the breadth of humanity.

> That was the Greek way of relieving the hardness and unspirituality of pure form. But it involved to a certain degree the sacrifice of what we call *expression*; and a system of abstraction which aimed always at the broad and general type, at the purging away from the individual of what belonged only to him, and of the mere accidents of a particular time and place, imposed upon the range of effects open to the Greek sculptor limits somewhat narrowly defined. (52)

In opposition to classical sculpture, the art of Michelangelo, Pater implies, is romantic, an expression of the inner life, the representation of individual sensibility. The system of Michelangelo represents a distinctly modern art. It is a culmination of the expressive sculpture of the Florentine Middle Ages, which in the Paterian history of artistic ideals occupies a midpoint between the incompleteness of Michelangelo and the *Allgemenheit* of the Greeks.

Although one would not likely realize it by reading Ruskin's lecture on Michelangelo, in the distinction between the Tuscan and Greek schools of sculpture, Ruskin and Pater are essentially in accord. Indeed, Pater's remarks in the essays on Luca and Michelangelo closely resemble Ruskin's analysis, in *Aratra Pentilici* (1870) and other

Oxford lectures, of the characteristic differences between the Greek and Florentine. The Greek never represents "expression," Ruskin emphasizes, while the Italian primarily seeks it. The Greek never represents "momentary passion," while to the Florentine it is "the ultimate object of his skill." The Greek never expresses "personal character," while to the Florentine it is "the ultimate condition of beauty."[15]

Pater deviates from Ruskin, not in his analysis of fifteenth-century expressive sculpture, but in his celebration of Michelangelo as the glorious culmination of that school. To Ruskin, Michelangelo's art marks the corruption and decay of the Florentine school, the point at which the dangers associated with an expressive aesthetic overtake and extinguish the particular strength of that art.

Four ৯ Romanticism and the
Oxford Lectures

W HEN Ruskin finally resigned as Slade Professor in 1885,
Pater put himself forward for the position. Not surprisingly, his candidacy was unsuccessful (the job went to Hu-
bert von Herkomer), but his desire to succeed Ruskin is another
indication that he was keenly aware of the older critic's presence at
Oxford. In this chapter I establish another, and previously unrecog-
nized, Pater-Ruskin correspondence—Pater's 1876 essay "Romanticism" and Ruskin's Oxford lecture, "Franchise," from the *Val D'Arno*
series, published in 1874. The texts represent each critic's fullest theoretical articulation of the term "romanticism," and demonstrate that
their respective theories justify distinct political ends and support different artistic values.

In 1883 Pater published yet another response to one of Ruskin's
Oxford lectures, his essay on Dante Gabriel Rossetti. Thomas Ward
asked Pater to contribute an introductory essay on Rossetti's poetry
for his *English Poets* anthology, and in a letter of March 5, 1883, Pater
put off giving him a definitive answer. Ruskin's announced lecture on
Rossetti was delivered on March 9, which suggests that Pater wanted
to hear Ruskin's talk before committing to his own essay. In his article,

"Pater's Aesthetic Poet: The Appropriation of Rossetti from Ruskin,"
Andrew Leng thoroughly demonstrates that Pater's essay "is shaped in
opposition to Ruskin's 1883 lectures on Pre-Raphaelitism" (Leng, 45),
so I will not rehearse again the details of the correspondence. But before turning to Pater's and Ruskin's specific treatments of "romanticism," I will summarize aspects of their responses to Rossetti germane
to my argument.

Rossetti

Ruskin inaugurated his second tenure as Slade Professor with a
series of lectures on modern English painting, later published as *The
Art of England*. Rossetti had died the preceding year and a retrospective
of his work was currently on exhibit at the Royal Academy. One of
Ruskin's aims, as he told friends, was to give "some permanently rational balance between the rhapsodies of praise and blame" (33:394)
that had followed Rossetti's death. He begins his first lecture, "Realistic Schools of Painting: D. G. Rossetti and W. Holman Hunt," by
identifying Rossetti as "the chief intellectual force in the establishment
of the modern romantic school" (33:269). "Those who are acquainted
with my former writings must be aware," Ruskin tells his audience,
"that I use the word 'romantic' always in a noble sense" (33:269), and
he loudly applauds Rossetti for instigating the nineteenth-century
revival of romance. But Ruskin's praise soon turns to disapproval, reflecting once again his deep ambivalence toward the modern romantic
revival. In the first part of the lecture Ruskin is full of praise for Rossetti, essentially repeating his earlier comments in *Modern Painters III*
(1856) and *The Three Colours of Pre-Raphaelitism* (1878). But suddenly,
and for the first time in public, Ruskin turns on the artist and accuses
him of what are by now the familiar modern sins of infidelity, insincerity, and disrespect for natural fact.

He begins by accusing Rossetti of infidelity: "To Rossetti, the Old
and New Testaments were only the greatest poem he knew; and he
painted scenes from them with no more actual belief in their relation

to the present life ... than he gave also the 'Morte d'Arthur' and the 'Vita Nuova'" (33:271). The criticism recalls his censure of Raphael's frescoes thirty years earlier in his lecture on "Pre-Raphaelitism"—"*he elevated the creations of fancy on the one wall, to the same rank as the objects of faith upon the other.*" Now that same criticism is being leveled at the founder of the Pre-Raphaelite school himself. Ruskin compares Rossetti unfavorably to his student Holman Hunt, who is "Beyond calculation, greater, beyond comparison, happier, than Rossetti, in his sincerity, he is distinguished also from him by a respect for physical and material truth which renders his work far more generally, far more serenely, exemplary" (33:271). In contrast to Hunt's "true representation of actual sunshine," Rossetti's sunshines are "unreal" and "perverted":

> Its light is not the light of sunshine itself, but of sunshine diffused through coloured glass. And in object-painting he not only refused ... refused, I say, the natural aid of pure landscape and sky, but wilfully perverted and lacerated his powers of conception with Chinese puzzles and Japanese monsters, until his foliage looked generally fit for nothing but a fire-screen, and his landscape distances like the furniture of a Noah's Ark from the nearest toy-shop. (33:271–72)

In Ruskin's analysis, Rossetti appears as a failed Pre-Raphaelite painter unable or unwilling to devote himself to the school's "primary virtue"—"the trying to conceive things as they are, and thinking and feeling them quite out" (33:290).

In his next lecture, "Mythic Schools of Painting: E. Burne-Jones and G. F. Watts," Ruskin explicitly excludes Rossetti from the "Mythic, or personifying" school. The lecture is devoted primarily to Burne-Jones, whom Ruskin identifies as the greatest modern painter of mythology. He differs "diametrically" from all other members of the Brotherhood in that his "essential gift and habit of thought is *in* personification" (33:292). Ruskin surprisingly turns to Rossetti to emphasize the contrast: "had both Rossetti and he been set to illustrate the first chapter of Genesis, Rossetti would have painted either Adam or Eve; but Edward Burne-Jones, a Day of Creation" (33:292).[1]

Pater's essay clearly challenges Ruskin's account of Rossetti, even though he directs his attention to the poetry. His watchwords are "sincerity" and "personification." Like Leonardo's and Wordsworth's, Rossetti's work is private, hermetic, and faithful to the picture within. "His own meaning was always personal and even recondite," Pater writes, "the just transcript of that peculiar phase of soul which he alone knew, precisely as he knew it" (*Appreciations*, 207). Rossetti becomes for Pater a paragon of the sincere writer who always strives to find the "exact equivalent" of the "*data* within" (206).

Moreover, in his passionate quest for sincerity, Rossetti is for Pater yet another modern master of the pathetic fallacy. He transforms "inanimate nature" into an intimate expression of soul: "For with Rossetti this sense of lifeless nature . . . is translated to a higher service, in which it does but incorporate itself with some phase of strong emotion" (*Appreciations*, 211). Pater describes his personifications as having a "hold upon him, with the force of Frankenstein" (208). So completely is Rossetti possessed by images of Death and Sleep or Love as living creatures, "with hands and eyes and articulate voices," that Pater notes in the poet's work that "insanity which follows a vivid poetic anthropomorphism," taking shape "in a forced and almost grotesque materialising of abstractions" (209). Ruskin, too, discerned a "certain feverishness of soul" in Rossetti. In contrast to Pater, however, feverishness impels Ruskin to exclude Rossetti from consideration as a "mythic" painter. Rossetti's Chinese puzzles and Japanese monsters fall short in Ruskin's critique, representing examples of the false grotesque.

Ruskin's Romanticism

Ten years before he turned on Rossetti, Ruskin set out his most explicit condemnation of modern romantic art and philosophy in his 1873 Oxford lecture "Franchise." It was published the next year in *Val*

D'Arno: Ten Lectures on the Tuscan Art Directly Antecedent to the Florentine Year of Victories. The book's subject is the glorious revival of the fine arts in Tuscany during the thirteenth century, but Ruskin is more concerned with tracing the social, political, and religious sources of the Florentine artistic revival. He makes an unfavorable comparison to thirteenth-century Florence, in which artisans and craftsmen were paid well for their daily work and encouraged to supply the best work that they could. It is impossible, Ruskin cries, "to overrate the difference between such a social condition, and that of the artists of to-day" who are "paid irregular and monstrous prices by an entirely ignorant and selfish public" and so compete with each other "to supply the worst article they can for the money" (23:49). The *Val D'Arno* lectures contain Ruskin's first public attack on Whistler, the type of modern artist, according to Ruskin, who doesn't know his business at all but whose daubing, "professing to be a 'harmony in pink and white' (or some such nonsense)" (23:49), commands a price of two hundred and fifty guineas.

"Franchise," the seventh lecture of the series, is a scathing attack on modern British culture, an attack Ruskin explicitly relates to his critique of modern romanticism. The lecture is based in an opposition between Greece and France for the sake of defining the differences between the classical and the romantic. In opposing Greece to France, Ruskin elaborates upon Gothic "Fury" and its subsequent "restraints of passion" by introducing and defining the term "franchise," given its first European expression, as its name indicates, in France. Modern art and culture, Ruskin argues, are a corruption of Gothic "franchise." As opposed to Greek "constancy," which characterizes the classical temper, Gothic "franchise" characterizes the romantic temper. Ruskin doesn't set one order of intelligence above the other—the classic and romantic "may be equally earnest, only different in manner" (23:134). Modern romantic art, however, is lacking in "franchise" and so is a perversion of the genuine romantic spirit.

Ruskin locates the Gothic in twelfth-century France, the seat of established Norman power and the source of Gothic franchise:

France is everlastingly, by birth, name, and nature, the country
of the Franks, or free persons; and the first source of European
frankness, or franchise. The Latin for franchise is libertas. But
the modern or Cockney-English word, liberty,—Mr. John Stuart Mill's,—is not the equivalent of libertas; and the modern or
Cockney-French word liberté,—M. Victor Hugo's,—is not the
equivalent of franchise. (23:116)

Romantic artists, Gothic or modern, express themselves under the
impulse of passions. This distinguishes them from the classical writers and painters who "set down nothing but what is known to be true
. . . and are thenceforward authorities from whom there is no appeal"
(23:122). The work of the romantic artist, conceived under the impulse
of passion, and often brilliant and beautiful, "remains imperfect, and
without authority" (23:122). The romantic artist always works under
the influence of passion, but this "unsystematic play of emotion"
(23:123) must be disciplined, governed by some degree of restraint (of
course, the argument echoes Ruskin's discussion of the pathetic fallacy). To be free, according to Ruskin's understanding of "franchise" or
"libertas," is to be capable of controlling the passions, "to be defiant
alike of the mob's thought, of the adversary's threat, and the harlot's
temptation" (23:117). The modern artist, Ruskin argues, rejects this ennobling restraint of emotion, thereby transforming "libertas" into the
dangerous modern notion of liberty, the liberty of John Stuart Mill.
Deficient in equity, compassion, medieval "largesse," modern romantic
art encourages self-sufficiency, chaos, and protest, the desire for eman-
cipation from any and all authority.

    Law is dominant over both the Greek and the Gothic, but the law
of each nation differs markedly from the other. Edward III obeys "the
law of love, *restraining* anger; but Theseus, slaying the Minotaur, is
obeying the law of justice, and *enforcing* anger" (23:117). What Ruskin
stresses, however, is that both the pure "discipline" and "judgment" of
the Greek and the pure "franchise" and "charity" of the Norman are to
be celebrated. The Greek represents "constancy" of body and thought,

the Gothic "franchise" of body and thought, one spirit informed by the Creed of St. Athanese, the other by St. Francis of Assisi.

> Utter franchise, utter gentleness in theological thought. Instead of, "This is the faith, which except a man believe faithfully, he cannot be saved," "This is the love, which if a bird or an insect keep faithfully, *it* shall be saved." (23:121)

Ruskin turns to the words of St. Francis and his strange and passionate extension of the doctrine of love and faith to include the heart and soul of a bird, to demonstrate the revision done to St. Athanese, one of Newman's favorites. But it is the modern rejection of both possibilities of the spirit that Ruskin deplores.

Having declared that modern life and art lack the virtue of both the Goth and the Greek, Ruskin proceeds to extend the differences that exist between these "two great nations" to the distinction that "exists also between two orders of intelligence among men" (23:121)—the classic, a result of Greek "constancy," and the romantic, a result of Gothic "franchise." The classic is characterized, according to Ruskin, by truth, flawlessness, and authority. The "writers and painters of the Classic school set down nothing but what is known to be true, and set it down in the perfectest manner possible in their way, and are thenceforward authorities from whom there is no appeal" (23:121–22). In contrast, the romantic is characterized by inconsistency and imperfection, despite its intensity and beauty. Romantic writers and painters

> express themselves under the impulse of passions which may indeed lead them to the discovery of new truths, or to the more delightful arrangement or presentment of things known: but their work, however brilliant or lovely, remains imperfect, and without authority. (23:122)

Ruskin's distinction between the classic and romantic closely resembles his earlier distinction between the Creative and Reflective orders of poets, and Ruskin maintains the same hierarchy between them. Like poets of the second or Reflective order, who are under the influence of emotion, "borne away, or over-clouded, or over-dazzled by emotion" (5:208), the Ruskinian romantic artist works under the impulse of passions, and his work, like that of the Reflective poet, however brilliant or lovely, is without authority. And as the distinct temperaments of the first and second orders of poets "are united each to the other by imperceptible transitions" (5:209), the same mind passing at different times into the opposing state, so is it impossible "trenchantly" to separate the classic from the romantic order of intelligence: "a classic writer may sometimes, whatever his care, admit an error, and a romantic one may reach perfection through enthusiasm" (23:122). For practical purposes, however, it is possible to separate the classic from the romantic, and Ruskin insists, for the same reasons that he chose Scott over Wordsworth as the representative poet of his age, that only classical books should be given to students to read in their youth, in order "to see that your minds are both informed of the indisputable facts they contain, and accustomed to act with the infallible accuracy of which they set the example" (23:122).

Gothic franchise in Ruskin's somewhat tortured analysis is only made possible by the Gothic impulse to passion in the first place, and this despite being characterized by control or government of the passions. He speaks of an "unsystematic play of emotion," which results in the creation of his ideal of romantic art. Yet even this unsystematic play, he claims, is governed by some degree of restraint in the Goth as well as by notions of right and wrong conduct. Consequently—at least for Ruskin it is a logical consequence—Gothic art can provide to its audience a kind of truth.

The romantic art of modern England, however, does not measure up, chiefly because it is not governed by any comparable notions of right conduct. The exception that proves the rule is—*quelle surprise!*—Walter Scott. Scott's character Diana Vernon from *Rob Roy* represents *libertas*, the ennobling control of the passions, a contrast to the unsystematic play of emotion and passion typically represented in modern art:

> Sir Walter's Franchise, Diana Vernon, interests you at once in
> personal aspect and character. She is no symbol to you; but if
> you acquaint yourself with her perfectly, you find her utter
> frankness, governed by a superb self-command; her spotless
> truth, refined by tenderness; her fiery enthusiasm, subdued by
> dignity; and her fearless liberty, incapable of doing wrong, join-
> ing to fulfil to you, in sight and presence, what the Greek could
> only teach by signs. (23:125)

Because Diana is characterized by "self-command," Ruskin points to
Scott's novel as an exalted romance. For Diana represents true franchise; it is her "conditions of purity and strength or spring which imply
the highest state of libertas" (23:125).

In contrast to Diana stands the heroine of Charles Reade's *Griffith
Gaunt*:

> By corruption of the idea of purity, you get the modern heroines
> of London Journal—or perhaps we may more fitly call it
> "Cockney-daily"—literature. You have one of them in perfec-
> tion, for instance, in Mr. Charles Reade's *Griffith Gaunt*—"Lithe,
> and vigorous, and one with her great white gelding"; and liable
> to be entirely changed in her mind about the destinies of her life
> by a quarter of an hour's conversation with a gentleman unex-
> pectedly handsome; the hero also being a person who looks at
> people whom he dislikes, with eyes "like a dog's in the dark"; and
> both hero and heroine having souls and intellects also precisely
> corresponding to those of a dog's in the dark, which is indeed
> the essential picture of the practical English national mind at
> this moment,—happy if it remains doggish,—Circe not usu-
> ally being content with changing people into dogs only. (23:125)

By way of conclusion, Ruskin notes that "what Diana Vernon is to a
French ballerine dancing the Cancan, the 'libertas' of Chartres and
Westminster is to the 'liberty' of M. Victor Hugo and Mr. John Stuart
Mill" (23:126).

Pater's Romanticism

Pater's "Romanticism" was originally published in November 1876, three years after Ruskin's lectures, but only two years after their publication. Pater later chose to include the essay, in a slightly revised form, as the last in *Appreciations*, renaming it "Postscript" and thereby offering it as something like a critical manifesto. Following Lionel Trilling, Harold Bloom suggests that Pater's essay is "an implicit reply" to Arnold's "The Study of Poetry," "opposing the criterion of 'energy' to Arnold's moral strictures" ("Crystal Man," 220). "Romanticism" is certainly a compelling reply, but it should be noted that it was originally published four years before Arnold's essay. I suggest, therefore, that Pater's original target was not Arnold, but the Slade Professor of Fine Art at Oxford.

It has also been proposed that "Romanticism" was Pater's response to W. J. Courthope's anonymous essay in the *Quarterly Review*, "Wordsworth and Gray," in which Wordsworth and the Romantics are heavily criticized.[2] As we saw in the introduction, Pater himself comes under explicit attack in Courthope's essay, representing the "emasculated principles" and solipsistic effect of romantic thought. Courthope distinguishes between the sensible classicism of Gray and the egotistical romanticism of Wordsworth, and Pater may very well have had Courthope's anonymous review in mind as he wrote his essay. As Inman says, by not mentioning Wordsworth, Pater implies "that anyone who traces the origin of Romanticism to Wordsworth, as Courthope had done, has a very provincial and quite erroneous understanding of the term" (*Pater's Reading*, 301).

As a literary and cultural critic, however, Ruskin was a far more pervasive presence than an anonymous reviewer of Wordsworth's poetry. More suggestively, Pater's essay specifically engages the ideas and images of Ruskin's "Franchise" lecture, constituting an important component of his response to Ruskin's critique of romanticism. Pater's essay begins by defining the "too absolute," and therefore "misleading" use of the words "classical" and "romantic." Although he certainly doesn't single out Ruskin by name, Pater directs his criticism toward the vague and "accidental" sense in which the term "romantic" is sometimes used by critics of Scott: "The sense in which Scott is called a romantic writer is chiefly that, in opposition to the literary tradition of the last century, he loved strange adventure, and sought it in the middle age" ("Romanticism," 64). Although granting the romance element in Scott, Pater finds him an equivocal exemplar of a romantic writer. Such a judgment, of course, directly opposes Ruskin. Pater points instead to Emily Brontë as a "more genuine fruit" (64) of romanticism. He calls attention to Heathcliff's tearing open Catherine's grave and climbing in beside her as typical of his ideal of romantic passion. Of course, such unrestrained conduct must appear in stark contradiction to Ruskin's notion of a "higher" romanticism made possible by the presence of "franchise" or "libertas." Scott's pure, dignified, and above all traditional Diana Vernon is entirely out of place in the Paterian romantic landscape inhabited by the wild Heathcliff and Catherine. Passion, rather than the ability to control it, becomes the hallmark of modern romanticism in Pater's reading of Brontë. One might object that a comparison of Heathcliff with Wordsworth, whom Pater has also identified with the romantic spirit, might seem extreme. But in fact I would argue that the same kind of passion born out of irrecoverable loss that moves Heathcliff to climb distractedly into that famed quiet grave moves Wordsworth to impassioned contemplation of an irrecoverable childhood.

Desire is at the foundation of the Paterian theory of romantic art. Heathcliff's strange passion is realized by means of Emily Brontë's desire for beauty. In Pater's theory, the desire for beauty exists in both classical and romantic art. But while the quest for perfect form characterizes the classical, "it is the addition of curiosity to this desire of beauty that constitutes the romantic temper" ("Romanticism," 65). In the Paterian lexicon curiosity seems to be synonymous with strangeness. If I am right about this then Pater's description of the romantic temper undergoes a subtle intensification, for when he talks about strangeness he calls it a "condition," not merely an "addition":

> With a passionate care for beauty, the romantic spirit refuses to
> have it, unless the condition of strangeness be first satisfied. Its
> desire is towards a beauty born of unlikely elements, by a pro-
> found alchemy, by a difficult initiation, by the charm which
> wrings it even out of terrible things; and a trace of distortion, of
> the grotesque, may perhaps linger, as an additional element of
> expression, about its ultimate grace. . . . Its eager, excited spirit
> will have strength, the grotesque, first of all—the trees shriek-
> ing as you tear off the leaves. (66)

The shrieking trees comes from Virgil's *Aeneid*. A more striking example of the pathetic fallacy would be difficult to find (indeed, is a
shrieking tree much different from a dancing leaf?). The obvious distortion of Virgil's image satisfies the condition of strangeness, allowing Pater to emphasize that the romantic spirit was present even in
the literature of Augustan Rome.

In the Paterian alchemy, the romantic spirit is tempered by
strangeness and intensified by restraint. Therefore, restraint becomes
an element of the successful evocation of romantic spirit. Significantly, Pater's formulation is reminiscent of Ruskin's idea that restraint is the crucial element of Gothic franchise and, in fact, is close
to the Ruskinian account of romantic intelligence. But where Ruskin
urges restraint as a means toward right conduct, Pater urges restraint
as aesthetic perfection. For Ruskin, restraint can result in the elimination of distortion; for Pater, restraint preserves distortion while pre-
venting it from decaying into the mere grotesque.[3]

The French Connection

As one of the finest and most representative examples of the romantic temper, Pater points to the French novelist Victor Hugo, the
target of so much of Ruskin's disdain and disapproval. Hugo stands
for Ruskin as the emblematic perversion of the romantic ideal; his
work promotes debased notions of liberty and passion rooted in the

dehumanizing conditions of the modern city. This is even more evident in his late series of essays, *Fiction, Fair and Foul*, published in between his two tenures as Slade Professor; there Ruskin vigorously
denounces the modern French novel and judges it the very type of
foul fiction, repository of idiocy, madness, horror, and mutilation.
Paris, Ruskin asserts, is the "central root" of this "literature of the
Prison-house," the supreme model of urban misery and degradation,
and Victor Hugo is its central representative—"the effectual head of
the whole cretinous school is the renowned novel in which the hunch-
backed lover watches the execution of his mistress from the tower of
Notre-Dame" (34:277).[4] In Pater's "Romanticism," Hugo's Quasimodo
represents that "certain distortion" that is a crucial element of the romantic, revealing "something of a terrible grotesque, of the *macabre*, as
the French themselves say—though always combined with perfect literary execution" ("Romanticism," 68). For Ruskin, in contrast, the
"cretinous" always marks a point beyond the limits of true romance.
Disease is never a fit subject for representation. Ruskin sees Hugo's
novel as a sick parody of the noble passion represented in the romances of the French Middle Age or in their most genuine modern
counterpart, the romances of Walter Scott. He describes the typical
novels of the modern French school as "Fiction mecroyante," referring
to their landscapes of the prison cell, the asylum, and the "dripping
slabs of the Morgue."

Ruskin's attack on French fiction reflects a pervasive Victorian
anxiety over the corrupting force of French influence, an anxiety Pater
consciously exploits in "Romanticism." Evident early in the century in
the *Blackwood's* attack on the Cockney School and its supposed sympathies with French revolutionary excess, this anti-French sentiment
reaches its apotheosis in Robert Buchanan's famous denunciation of
the Pre-Raphaelites as a Fleshly School of Poetry (Dowling, *Hellenism
and Homosexuality*, 1–31). Buchanan traces the sins of Swinburne and
Rossetti to Baudelaire, the locus of modern poetry's "unnatural passion," "blasphemy," and "wretched animalism" (*Fleshly School*, 16–32).
Throughout the century, French fiction is condemned from pulpits

and in periodical reviews as a licentious influence sanctioning adultery and divorce (Decker; Houghton, 359–68). On the one hand, Pater seeks to reverse the provincial prejudice of his countrymen and foster a sympathetic appreciation of French literature.[5] More strategically, however, he draws on the deeply ingrained British fear of French influence to link his theory of romanticism with the exotic, the erotic, and the avant-garde. Pater's alignment of romanticism with nineteenth-century French literature signals to his contemporaries the radical cultural value he attaches to romanticism. Despite the genteel tone and the effort to defuse the romantic-classic opposition, Pater's essay is deliberately provocative and polemical. His theory of romanticism stands in opposition not to classicism—the category to which all romantic art, if it is good enough, is destined—but to the Victorian forces of antiliberalism that would limit the freedom of both artist and non-artist and impose narrow standards of taste and conduct.[6]

One can detect strains of this same polemic in Pater's celebration of the French Gothic. Pater celebrates its expression of unrestrained desire and emotion, the beginning of a strange and new artistic spirit. Given Ruskin's admiration of Gothic restraint, it is difficult not to read Pater as a conscious rebuke of his older contemporary.

> Here, in the poetry of Provence, the very name of romanticism is stamped with its true signification; here we have indeed a romantic world, grotesque even, in the strength of its passions, almost insane in its curious expression of them, drawing all things into its sphere, making birds and lifeless things its voices and messengers; yet so penetrated with the desire for beauty and sweetness, that it begets a wholly new species of poetry, in which the *Renaissance* may be said to begin. ("Romanticism," 67)

The poetry of the French Middle Ages is "almost insane" in its animistic expression, its unrestrained narcissism giving voice to a vision of the natural world peopled with the spirits of human beings. The romantic temper of Pater's French Middle Ages reaches its zenith in an utter loosing of the passions, a liberty made possible through the release, rather than the restraint, of desire.

According to Pater, in the midst of the French classical period the seeds of nineteenth-century romanticism were planted. Pater identifies Rousseau as the beginning of modern French romanticism. The most influential source of the romantic spirit's eruption in the nineteenth century is the terrible tragedy of Rousseau, whose *Confessions* "anticipate all the Werthers, Renes, Obermanns, of the last hundred years" ("Romanticism," 68). Rousseau introduces to French literature a strong, disturbing, yet irresistible quality that is characteristic of romantic invention. "His passionateness, his lacerated heart, his deep subjectivity, his *bizarrerie*, his distorted strangeness—he makes all men in love with these" (67).

Rousseau is not alone, however. Pater allows that other eighteenth-century writers also demonstrate the romantic qualities that will become "the habitual guise" of the next century, including Oliver Goldsmith, the Irish poet whom Ruskin singled out in his "Franchise" lecture as a quintessential "classical" author. Ruskin read to his audience fifty-two lines from *The Deserted Village* that, in his words, "contain more truth than has been told you all this year by this whole globe's compass of print" (23:122). By characterizing Goldsmith as pre-romantic, Pater is overturning Ruskin's appropriation of the poet as a classical author.

Liberating Romanticism

Pater's essay liberates romanticism from the moral and authoritarian strictures of Ruskin's "libertas," aligning the romantic spirit with the liberty of John Stuart Mill and the liberal conviction in the individual's freedom of thought.[7] Pater's valorization of individual desire places him in concert with late Victorian liberalism and its claims for liberty, individuality, self-development, and diversity. As I pointed out in the introduction, scholars have recently argued that in much of his work Pater in fact radicalizes Victorian liberal assumptions inasmuch as he tries to establish homosexuality as a positive social identity. I am suggesting, therefore, that Pater's writings on romanticism complement the sociopolitical aspirations of Oxford Hellenism and its coded homosexual counterdiscourse. This counterdiscourse, promoting liberal assumptions while ambushing the liberal discourse of masculinity, is a constant undercurrent in Pater's work as it has been interpreted by Linda Dowling, Richard Dellamora, and others. For Pater, Ruskin's idea of a true romanticism defined by franchise is false and repressive, a vestige of Tory republicanism to which Pater's reception of romanticism is in conscious opposition.

Pater's homosexual counterdiscourse is a critique from within liberalism. For this reason we can read his well-known celebration of romantic subjectivity as a promotion of Victorian liberal ideals. As we have seen, for Pater Rousseau's famous words from the *Confessions* inspire nineteenth-century romanticism: "I am not made like any one else I have ever known: yet, if I am not better, at least I am different." Pater points to Rousseau's emphasis on difference as an essential characteristic of the romantic spirit. As opposed to classical art, which possesses the "charm of familiarity" and the power to "tranquillise us," romantic art has the ability to excite us, to provide new and curious impressions and pleasures. "All good art was romantic in its day," writes Pater, referring to Stendahl's argument in his *Racine and Shakespeare*, and the object of Stendahl's book, Pater tells us, "is to defend the liberty and independence of choice, and treatment of subject, in art and literature, against those who uphold the exclusive authority of precedent" ("Romanticism," 69). The romanticist demands novelty, and in his craving for "new motives, new subjects of interest, new modifications of style," he is the adherent of liberty and strength. His temper is defined by curiosity, which naturally tends toward strangeness, the bizarre or *recherché* that is the romantic element in art. This "romantic condition of strangeness" shows itself in the traces of distortion that linger about romantic art, for distortion reveals the unique temperament and point of view of the artist.

Pater implies that romantic subjectivity, passion, and curiosity are liberal concepts because they support the autonomy and self-development of the individual, and in making these claims for romanticism Pater undergirds and even radicalizes Victorian liberal doctrine. In doing this he is a proponent of modern life, in direct opposition to Ruskin. Pater's romanticism is an avant-garde movement, always reflecting the spirit of the age and following the movements of the ever-changing *Zeitgeist*. As such, the romantic spirit embraces modern life with all of its bewildering complexity and social transformations. The romanticist cultivates the relative spirit, which is for Pater the defining characteristic of modern thought, for he is a passionate individualist and rejects all forms of the absolute. He is, in Pater's words, "the progressive element in [his] own generation" (69).

Pater argues that the moral consequence of romantic subjectivity is a deepened tendency toward sympathy, not hubris or social indifference, as Ruskin feared. Pater's emphasis on sympathy as a source of moral feeling and action is consistent with his liberal defense of the individual and of the relative spirit. For a morality that is all sympathy, as Pater says of Botticelli, is an exceedingly flexible form of moral judgment: "[T]he habit of noting and distinguishing one's own most intimate passages of feeling, makes one sympathetic, as begetting a keen habit of entering . . . into the intimate recesses of other minds. So that pity is a note of romanticism" (68). In effect, Pater rejects the Ruskinian or Arnoldian opposition between egotism and sympathy, arguing instead that romantic subjectivity enhances the powers of sympathy. Pater contends that romanticism inculcates tolerance and this links him inextricably with the program of Victorian liberalism. As representative of romanticism's sympathetic pathos, Pater points to Victor Hugo and Charles Baudelaire. Hugo, Pater writes, "turns romanticism back into practice, in his hunger and thirst after *Justice!*—a justice which shall no longer wrong, by ignoring them in a stupid, mere breadth of view, facts about animals and children. Yet they are antinomian, too, sometimes" (68). In citing the theological concept of "antinomianism," which is the replacement by faith of obedience to a moral law, Pater secularizes the concept, aligning faith with the romantic spirit. The romantic spirit can be seen both in Hugo's justice/moral law and in the loosening of that law. This is where Pater opposes Ruskin, for whom there can never be a loosening or an abrogation of the moral law.

Both Pater and Ruskin invoke the antinomian spirit of romanticism, but Ruskin finally bridles and wants to check that antinomian spirit with a Tory authoritarianism, mystified as a kind of natural prudent restraint in the Frank. Pater responds by rejecting Ruskin's notion of franchise and arguing that the antinomian spirit can be nurtured to produce a deeper sympathy and wider identity with diverse aspects and categories of society. Most likely Pater encourages this antinomianism from a sociopolitical perspective because it helps him to resist the political status quo under which his own sexuality had to be repressed. He directly engages Ruskin on the subject of liberty and, interestingly, this engagement plays itself out in competing theories of romanticism.

Pater is always both urbane and oblique, at times even deliberately elitist. We never find him, for instance, campaigning for universal suffrage or for improving the working conditions for industrial and agricultural laborers. We do see, however, that in his defense of romanticism, and in confrontation with Ruskin, Pater endorses liberal aims, implying that individual differences of all kinds should be the subject of tolerance and sympathy. When Pater decided to close *Appreciations* with the essay "Romanticism" he appended to it a final paragraph in which he directly addresses the artists of his day: "Material for the artist," Pater counsels, "motives of inspiration, are not yet exhausted: our curious, complex, aspiring age still abounds in subjects for aesthetic manipulation by the literary as well as by other forms of art" (*Appreciations*, 260). Rejoice, Pater urges, in what is surely a rejoinder to critics like Ruskin and Arnold, in the eclecticism and diversity of our "intellectually rich age," for "in literature as in other matters it is well to unite as many diverse elements as may be" (261).

Conclusion

EVIDENTLY Pater's rescue of romanticism failed. Since Pater's day, theories attacking or defending romanticism have continued unabated. I think, however, that while the rescue efforts continue, we can view the Pater-Ruskin opposition as a cornerstone of Anglo-American disagreements over the nature and value of romanticism. There are Continental arguments that antedate Pater and Ruskin, and Marxist-inspired arguments that postdate them; moreover, the complications of twentieth-century criticism cannot be traced to any one source. But Ruskin's ambivalent critique and Pater's attempt at rescue remain to a large degree paradigmatic of subsequent theories of romanticism.

Recently, Marxist and New Historicist critiques have cast romanticism as an aesthetic ideology that suppresses history. Key to these critiques is the notion that in romantic poetry social and economic realities are displaced by a putative purity of consciousness.[1] We might, then, regard the new historicist theory of romanticism as an elaborate reformulation of Ruskin's pathetic fallacy, which was a similar protest against romantic poetry's displacement of realities.[2] Pater's defense of that displacement, his advocacy of the romantic artist's projective consciousness, places him squarely within the romantic ideology as

McGann defines it (Williams, 80) and aligns him with the "idealist, imagination-privileging" criticism of the 1960s and 1970s to which the new historicist critique is opposed (Bate, 6).

It also establishes him as the first literary theorist in England to attempt an explicit defense against the accusations that romanticism promotes egotism and a disregard of social life. As we have seen, Pater converts what Ruskin judges to be intemperate passion into a heightened sense of sympathy and pity, thereby rescuing what Ruskin condemns in romantic practice. Again and again, in the essays on Wordsworth, Leonardo, Rossetti, and Morris, Pater manages to figure the pathetic fallacy as that very means of connectedness to the world to which Ruskinian art also aspires.

Pater's transformation of the defining trope of romantic literature into a vision of shared human feeling is consistent with his efforts to establish a theory of romanticism in support of liberal values. Subsequent theories seeking to align romanticism with the political desire for personal freedom, especially those defined in opposition to the antiromantic enthusiasm of the years leading up to World War II, resonate strongly with Pater's rhetoric. The antiromantic critics of the early twentieth century, including T. S. Eliot, Irving Babbitt, Yvor Winters, Allen Tate, Albert Guerard, and Peter Viereck, ranged widely in their interests and emphases. But they shared the conviction that romantic philosophy promoted a wrongheaded, adolescent notion of liberty. In his 1919 *Rousseau and Romanticism*, Babbitt characterized Ruskin as the quintessential romantic, an English echo of Rousseau's arrogance, his "feminine . . . preference for illusion" (158), and his "emotional misanthropy" (279). But Babbitt's endless depictions of the romantic's weak "inner check," his utter lack of any principle of control, recall Ruskin's vision of the modern perversion of franchise and the lack of Gothic restraint.

Against the Humanist and New Critical antiromantic onslaught, a great many critics set out to revalue the romantic achievement, emphasizing what they believed were the positive social, political, and cultural consequences of romantic art and philosophy. Foremost among them was the eminent historian Jacques Barzun, who in 1940 published a brief essay in *The American Scholar* titled "To the Rescue of Romanticism." I have borrowed Barzun's title for my study because Barzun's defense of romanticism is, in its key points, strikingly analogous with Pater's.

Barzun's most direct targets were those critics who associated romanticism with the antirational idealism of Hitler and Mussolini, a judgment that would culminate one year later in the publication of Peter Viereck's *Metapolitics: From the Romantics to Hitler* (1941). In opposition, Barzun characterizes what he terms the romantic "temper" as committed to social relativity, diversity, democracy, and the historical method.

> Perceiving all forms and conventions to be relative, the romanticist is an individualist, a democrat and a cosmopolitan. Having had the mutability of human affairs brought home to him and being endowed with the spirit of adventure, he values the variety of human experience. As artist he seeks to capture local color; as historian he distinguishes the genius of many lands or peoples; as natural scientist he pleads for the method of observation without moral judgment; as philosopher he shows how very narrow are the limits of pure reason. (149–50)

We hear in Barzun's rhetoric the specific argument, even the cadence, of Pater's "Romanticism." Barzun defines democracy in terms that resonate with Pater's essay: "equality in diversity . . . the recognition of difference and the tolerance that goes with it" (154). Barzun endorses the romantic embrace of "the historical method . . . the distrust of absolute, *a priori* reasoning" (154), and he identifies the romantic with a genuine, fervent spirituality, "inexhaustible passion," and "unconcealed restlessness" (151). Pater's rescue of romanticism was far less conspicuous than that attempted by Barzun. But it is equally inspired by the pursuit of specific political ideals and literary values. Barzun's defense of romanticism, linking democracy and tolerance to an aesthetic movement, constitutes the fruit of which Pater's response to Ruskin is the seed.

This image of Pater may strike some readers as counterintuitive. He is far more widely regarded as having helped inspire the New Humanist and New Critical indictment of romanticism than as having provided a defense against it. In his 1911 review of the Library Edition, for instance, P. E. More grouped Pater with those "modern romantics" who reinforce "the romantic ideal of the imagination as a worship of beauty isolated from, and in the end despised by, the real interests of life" (Seiler, 422). "Paterism," More concludes, "might without great injustice be defined as the quintessential spirit of Oxford, emptied of the wholesome intrusions of the world" and characterized by "sterile self-absorption," "a faint Epicureanism," and "voluptuous economy of sensations" (Seiler, 422). T. S. Eliot's disdain for Pater is similarly keen. For Eliot, Pater represented the most dangerous type of critic, the romantic, self-indulgent impressionist whose confusion of art with life was responsible for some "untidy lives." Barzun's defense of romantic passion and restlessness, therefore, is in large part an effort to undo the seamy, unwholesome image of the romantic that Pater himself, especially in his early essays, helped create and perpetuate. We might even say that Barzun rescues Pater and romanticism at the same time.

No essay of Pater's presents a wilder or stranger image of the romantic than his significant early attempt to theorize romanticism, the 1868 "Poems by William Morris." The essay offers a less mature theory than the 1876 "Romanticism," but it is already a development from the 1866 Coleridge essay. Pater associates romanticism not with "home sickness" and "languor" as he had with Coleridge ("Coleridge's Writings," 60), but with "the inversion of homesickness . . . that incurable thirst for the sense of escape" ("Poems by William Morris," 144). Rebellion replaces ennui as the pervading spirit of the romantic. In the Morris essay, Pater repeatedly and dramatically associates romanticism with transgression, license, the actual crossing of limits. The romantic revival itself, of which Morris's poetry is a "refinement," begins as a reaction against the "outworn classicism" of the eighteenth century.

As opposed to the romanticism essay, in which Pater describes the romantic as "an ever-present tendency," the history of romanticism presented in the Morris essay is more discrete, although complex. Pater divides the romantic revival into two historical currents, medieval and ancient, and then further divides romantic medievalism into two phases, an older medieval revival described as "superficial," full of "adventure," "romance in the poorest sense," and a "later, profounder medievalism," more passionate, mystical, above all rebellious. As yet a further "refinement" of this more profound medievalism, Morris's poetry belongs securely in the "romantic school," which, Pater declares, "mark[s] a transition not so much from the pagan to the medieval ideal, as from a lower to a higher degree of passion in literature" ("Poems by William Morris," 144).[3]

Building on the art historical analysis of "Winckelmann," Pater's description of this later phase of medievalism is outrageously anti-Ruskinian. The account of Gothic sensuousness and unrestrained passion is itself wildly unrestrained, far more excessive and dramatic than the analogous portrait of the French Gothic in "Romanticism." Pater's anti-Christian sentiment is nowhere more explicitly asserted, except perhaps in the Coleridge essay.[4] Pater argues that Provençal poetry functions in medieval life as a purposeful and powerful antagonist to Christianity, offering "a deliberate choice between Christ and a rival lover" ("Poems by William Morris," 144). Romanticism is figured as a sexual and sensual revolution. The imaginative loves of the Provençal poets constitute "a rival religion" with a "new rival cultus. . . . Coloured through and through with Christian sentiment, they are rebels against it" (144).

Most readers of Pater know that the "Conclusion" to *The Renaissance* was originally published as the second part of the 1868 essay on Morris. We tend to overlook, however, that in its original context Pater's exhortation to spend our interval in high passions, to get as many pulsations as possible into the given time, immediately follows the analysis of Morris and romanticism (Brake, *Walter Pater*, 20). Pater explicitly linked his philosophy of life to the romantic school, as did his contemporary readers. As we saw in the introduction, W. J. Courthope groups Pater with the modern "apologists of romanticism" ("Wordsworth and Gray," 70) and regards the "Conclusion" as the zenith of romantic decadence: "What wonder, if Mr. Pater's taste is good, that Mr. Swinburne should dilate on the beauty of hermaphrodites, and grow rapturous over the 'luxurious lovingness' of snakes!" (70). P. E. More and then T. S. Eliot and the "Cambridge critics" continue the attack on Pater's corrupt romantic affinities. Eliot accuses Pater of immorality and excessive weariness. More assails what he perceives as Pater's perverse morbidity.

Precisely against comments such as these, and in defense of writers such as Pater, Barzun performs his rescue of romanticism. The character of that rescue, however, was already established by Pater himself. Pater turns to modern art as the paladin of what he calls a sense of freedom, what Barzun—and we—call individualism:

> What modern art has to do in the service of culture is so to rearrange the details of modern life, so to reflect it, that it may satisfy the spirit. And what does the spirit need in the face of modern life? The sense of freedom. . . . Can art represent men and women in these bewildering toils so as to give the spirit at least an equivalent for the sense of freedom? (Pater, "Winckelmann," 50)

Notes

Introduction: The Rescue of Romanticism

1. All references to Ruskin's work will be cited in the text by volume and page number from the Library Edition, *The Works of John Ruskin*, edited by Cook and Wedderburn. For a study of Ruskin's Evangelical faith as it influences his response to the natural world, see C. Stephen Finley, *Nature's Covenant: Figures of Landscape in Ruskin*.

2. The major studies of Pater's relation to modernism are Perry Meisel, *The Myth of the Modern: A Study in British Literature and Criticism after 1850*, and F. C. McGrath, *The Sensible Spirit: Walter Pater and the Modernist Paradigm*. Gerald Monsman's "Pater and His Younger Contemporaries" and *Walter Pater* are the earliest studies of Pater's influence on the moderns, but there are numerous other books and articles establishing and suggesting Pater's relation to Yeats, Woolf, Joyce, Eliot, Pound, James, Conrad, Stevens, Ashberry, Cassirer, Borges, Beckett, Robbe-Grillet, Nabokov, Fowles, Barth, Barthelme, Proust, Poulet, Benjamin, Derrida, de Man, and Bloom, among others. I have taken this list from Shuter (*Rereading Pater*, 139).

3. There are of course exceptions, most notably Peter Allan Dale, *The Victorian Critic and the Idea of History: Carlyle, Arnold, Pater*; David DeLaura, *Hebrew and Hellene in Victorian England: Newman, Arnold, and Pater*; Frank Kermode, *The Romantic Image*; and Graham Hough, *The Last Romantics*.

4. My use of the word "conservative" is not meant to be politically restrictive, but is simply meant as a loose opposition to the typical Victorian liberal

concerns. As his readers have long recognized, even this loose opposition breaks down in Ruskin's political writing.

5. Other conceptual problems identified by Hassan that apply to the categorical term "romanticism" include the necessity of "both historical and theoretical definition," as well as the questions of whether it is "only an artistic tendency or also a social phenomenon" and whether it is "a descriptive as well as evaluative or normative category of literary thought" (149–51).

6. Whether or not romanticism constitutes a unified movement or phenomenon has been a central question in twentieth-century romantic scholarship. In his 1924 essay, "On the Discrimination of Romanticisms," A. O. Lovejoy famously declared that the "word 'romantic' has come to mean so many things that, by itself, it means nothing. It has ceased to perform the function of a verbal sign" (232). Lovejoy characterized romanticism by its plurality and set out to discriminate one romanticism from another. In his response to Lovejoy, René Wellek argued for the unity and coherence of romanticism, which he described as a set of cultural phenomena unified by similar conceptions of the poetic imagination, of nature and its relation to humanity, and of poetic style. See Wellek's "Periods and Movements in Literary History" and "The Concept of Romanticism in Literary History." Wellek's formulation was particularly influential and is the basis for recent attacks on romanticism as an "ideology." Despite the present emphasis on the contingencies of historical narrative, however, the notion of romanticism as a unified movement or period remains a powerful assumption in the critical literature. See Mark Parker's essay, "Measure and Countermeasure: The Lovejoy-Wellek Debate and Romantic Periodization," in which he traces the "inexpungeable presence" in recent accounts of romanticism "of the critical framework set out by the Wellek/Lovejoy debate" (238).

7. Sayre and Lowy represent one of the few recent attempts to describe romanticism as a coherent phenomenon. Their essay attempts, from a Marxist perspective, an analysis of romanticism as a *Weltanschauung*, defined by "opposition to capitalism in the name of precapitalist values" (24).

8. Although the distinction was not neglected. See Weisinger, who determines that "discussion of the differences between classical and romantic occurs in the work of Coleridge, Hazlitt, Scott, Robinson, and De Quincey, with the bulk of exposition centering in Coleridge and De Quincey" (479). Nevertheless, the material "occupies a relatively small part in the bulk of their collected writings" and "there is a complete silence on the subject" in the writing of their contemporaries, which Weisinger speculates is due either to a "lack of interest in the discussion or . . . an active dislike of it" (487).

9. Exceptions include Christian Willerton's dissertation, "A Study of Walter

Pater's *Appreciations*," and some brief comments in Buckler (171–76). The best account of Pater's relation to the romantic tradition is Peter Allan Dale's chapter, "Historicism and the Hellenic Ideal" (206–45). See also Bloom ("Crystal Man," vii–xxxi; "Place of Pater," 185–96); O'Hara (9–54); and Conlon (*Pater and the French Tradition*, 71–105).

10. See also Courthope's anonymous essay, "Modern Culture" (389–415) and his book, *The Liberal Movement in English Literature*. "I might, indeed, have called the series 'The Romantic Movement in English Literature,'" Courthope wryly remarks in the book's introduction (viii). Courthope's attacks on romanticism mirror Ruskin's arguments, although they are arrived at by a very different route.

11. I take the term from Dowling's *Hellenism and Homosexuality*.

12. Other models of expressive critical prose available to Pater include Hazlitt, Lamb, and Coleridge. Pater, of course, published essays on Lamb and Coleridge, but never mentions Hazlitt either in print or in his letters.

13. As a number of critics have suggested, this leads Ruskin to value allegory above symbol or metaphor in his theory of figure, for allegory declares its own fictiveness, thereby skirting the dangers of epistemological confusion. "When the imagination deceives, it becomes madness. It is a noble faculty so long as it confesses its own ideality; when it ceases to confess this, it is insanity. All the difference lies in the fact of the confession, in their [*sic*] being *no* deception. It is necessary to our rank as spiritual creatures, that we should be able to invent and behold what is not; and to our rank as moral creatures, that we should know and confess at the same time that it is not" (8:58). See especially Sprinker ("Ruskin on the Imagination"; *Imaginary Relations*, 11–34) and Wihl, *Ruskin and the Rhetoric of Infallibility*.

14. Published in *The Oxford Magazine*, 25 February 1885. I am grateful to Billie Andrew Inman for this reference.

15. Following Pater's own description of Raphael, Inman describes Pater as a "genius by accumulation" and a "brilliant original who did not originate" (*Pater's Reading*, xxix). In her two-volume study of Pater's reading, Inman traces his ideas to Kant, Goethe, Fichte, Berkeley, Hegel, Renan, Sainte-Beuve, Michelet, Quinet, Hume, and Bacon, among many, many others.

16. William Sharp reports that it was "a joy" for Pater to have in his possession, even on loan, an autographed manuscript of a prose passage by Ruskin (187–228).

17. Of course, neither Ruskin nor Pater was the first Englishman, much less the first critic, to write appreciatively of Botticelli. See Michael Levey, "Botticelli and Nineteenth-Century England."

18. Bloom attributes Pater's enormous influence on modernism to the

compromise he effects between Wordsworth and Ruskin, "de-idealizing" Wordsworth's "spots of time" while simultaneously transforming Ruskin's pathetic fallacies into "triumphs of perception" ("Crystal Man," x–xv).

19. His analysis, therefore, also extends to the presence of Ruskin in Pater's fiction. See also Solomon Fishman, *The Interpretation of Art: Essays on the Art Criticism of John Ruskin, Walter Pater, Clive Bell, Roger Fry, and Herbert Read,* and G. Robert Stange, "Art Criticism as a Prose Genre." In a related project, Lee McKay Johnson has examined both critics' literary response to painting, along with that of Baudelaire and Proust, as an important step in the development of Symbolism, emphasizing Pater's codification and transformation of Ruskin (Johnson, *Metaphor of Painting*).

20. See also the notes to Donald L. Hill's edition of *The Renaissance.*

21. Bizup focuses primarily on Pater's *Marius the Epicurean.* In *Masculine Desire,* Richard Dellamora discusses Pater's positive representation of Leonardo's "sexual perversity" as a response to Ruskin's troubled reflections on the character of male artistic genius (117–29).

22. The Keefes emphasize Pater's engagement with Ruskin throughout their book. The last chapter is a reading of Pater's "Apollo in Picardy" as a veiled portrait of Ruskin. James Kissane ("Victorian Mythology") and Steven Connor ("Myth as Multiplicity") both suggest that Pater's mythological theory resembles Ruskin's three-phase model from *The Queen of the Air.* Inman disagrees, finding Pater's ideas on myth more "complicated" than Ruskin's. She traces Pater's "three phases" theory of myth to Schiller's aesthetic theory, especially *On the Aesthetic Education of Man* (Inman, *Pater and His Reading,* 176–78).

23. Among others, Jay Fellows (*Tombs, Despoiled and Haunted*), Wolfgang Iser (*Walter Pater*), and Carolyn Williams (*Transfigured World*) have made important observations regarding Pater's revision of Ruskin's aesthetic theory.

24. The most theoretically rigorous expression of the desire to preserve the identity of the author while still maintaining poststructuralist insights into textuality is made by recent feminist theorists. Critics such as Nancy K. Miller, Margaret Homans, Mary Poovey, and Linda Alcoff resist the orthodox discourse of anonymous intertextuality, what Foucault calls "transcendental anonymity" (120), for it tends to eclipse any politics of identity in favor of an impersonal cultural text that produces or even authorizes all social change or rebellion. See Susan Stanford Friedman, "Weavings: Intertextuality and the (Re)Birth of the Author" for a discussion of Miller's efforts in *Subject to Change* to "separate the concept of intertextuality from the death of the author" (Friedman, 159). See also Homans, *Bearing the Word: Language and Female Experience in Nineteenth-Century Women Writers;* Poovey, "Feminism and Deconstruction"; and Alcoff, "Cultural Feminism versus Post-Structuralism: The Identity Crisis in Feminist Theory."

Chapter One: The Wordsworth of Pater and Ruskin

1. Because I am reading Pater's texts in relation to Ruskin I usually refer to the original published versions of the essays rather than to the revised version in *Appreciations* or *Studies in the History of the Renaissance*.

2. I disagree with Inman's assertion that "To Pater, Wordsworth was not Romantic" (*Pater and His Reading*, 301). Even she seems to qualify the claim when in another note she writes that "for Pater Wordsworth represents expression of only the 'healthier' aspects of Romanticism—fundamental, human emotions, the tie between nature and human beings, and the power of nature to instruct and delight" (53). Ultimately she suggests that Pater distinguishes "Wordsworthian pastoral" from "Romanticism," and that Wordsworth was too much concerned with the *"fundamental* emotions of humanity" for Pater to consider him romantic (301). I think she underestimates the strangeness of Pater's Wordsworth.

3. See Jeffrey Spear's *Dreams of an English Eden: Ruskin and His Tradition in Social Criticism* for a discussion of the romance structure of Ruskin's social vision.

4. My analysis of Ruskin's reception of Wordsworth owes much to Helsinger's study, in which she identifies two very different attitudes in Ruskin's critical response to the poet: his "highly critical attitude toward Wordsworth as a romantic poet of imagination and his great admiration of him as a guide in reforming perception." As she suggests, "the relationship between the two attitudes is more dialectical than contradictory" (6).

5. As Stephen Prickett explains, "for many Victorians Wordsworth *was* preeminently a religious poet. If he spoke to Mill and Arnold, both . . . bystanders, outside the rigid dogmatic framework of institutionalised religion, he had also a profound and lasting effect on natural dissenters like Mark Rutherford and George MacDonald, on Evangelicals such as Kingsley and Hughes, determined non-party men like F. D. Maurice, and through Keble, perhaps the greatest Wordsworthian of them all, on the whole Oxford Movement including Pusey and Newman" (71).

6. From a letter to his father, December 14, 1851.

7. All references to Wordsworth's poetry will be cited in the text by line number and are from *William Wordsworth: The Poems*, edited by John O. Hayden.

8. The extent of the shift in Ruskin's religious thought remains a subject of critical debate. As Michael Wheeler points out in his new book, *Ruskin's God*, critics have tended to perpetuate "the myth of Ruskin's catastrophic and irrecoverable 'loss of faith,' a myth which he himself invented in a sense in his descriptions of the 'Queen of Sheba crash' in Turin in 1858" (xiii). While Wheeler details the "many changes" in Ruskin's religious beliefs, he argues, definitively I think,

that Ruskin never lost "belief in divine wisdom and a God of peace" (xv). Wheeler argues that this belief was nurtured throughout his career "by his imaginative engagement with the peaceable Solomon and Old Testament wisdom literature" (278).

9. I take the phrase from Paul de Man, who argues in his essay "Wordsworth and the Victorians" that the self-reflecting Wordsworth is a product of the twentieth century, conceived "in parallel with the development of phenomenological and existential modes of thought" (86). In this sense, his argument is consistent with Finley. Victorian critics understood Wordsworth, de Man contends, "as a moral philosopher," with the "power to console, to edify, and to protect from anxieties that threaten life and reason" (85). The inward, self-reflecting Wordsworth was only barely perceptible to Victorian readers. "The best contemporary criticism is attuned to this inner voice that Victorian didacticism could only perceive at a muted distance" (87).

10. Harrison specifies texts as diverse as *Aurora Leigh, David Copperfield*, Tennyson's "The Two Voices" and *In Memoriam*, Browning's "Cleon" and "Asolando," and Arnold's *Empedocles*, "The Scholar-Gypsy," and "Thyrsis."

11. *The Poems of Tennyson*, edited by Christopher Ricks.

12. All references to Arnold's prose will be cited in the text by volume and page number from *The Complete Prose Works of Matthew Arnold*, edited by R. H. Super.

13. Antony Harrison points out that in his later years Swinburne shifted in his "ideological" evaluation of the older poet. "By the 1880s . . . as Swinburne's own productions became more politically conservative, indeed often xenophobic and jingoistic, his appropriations of Wordsworth become visibly less subversive" (184). For a discussion of Swinburne's assessment of both Wordsworth and Arnold's reaction to Wordsworth see Thaïs E. Morgan, "Rereading Nature: Wordsworth between Swinburne and Arnold." For further and more detailed examples of Swinburne's response to the "Intimations" ode, see Harrison's reading of "On the Downs" (*Victorian Poets*, 194–99), and David Riede's analysis of "On the Cliffs" and "By the North Sea," in *Swinburne: A Study of Romantic Mythmaking* (138–86).

14. In a note to the 1883 edition Ruskin defines his use of the word "type" as "any character in material things by which they convey an idea of immaterial ones" (4:76).

15. From the headnote to the "Intimations" ode.

16. As Carolyn Williams maintains, summing up the philosophical implications of the "Conclusion," Pater "pushes the literary tradition of romantic epistemology further toward its limits by figuratively expressing the danger as even more acute, reflexive, and involuted" (21).

17. For further discussions of the cozy Victorian "Daddy Wordsworth" see Carl Woodring, "Wordsworth and the Victorians" (261–75), and Paul de Man, "Wordsworth and the Victorians."

18. As J. P. Ward remarks, the comments on Wordsworth in the "Preface" are "oddly irrelevant" if "Wordsworth" was not originally intended to be part of *The Renaissance* (Ward, 66). See also Crawford (867–76).

19. In his 1883 introductory note, Ruskin dismisses the imagination-fancy distinction as a youthful indiscretion: "The reader must be warned not to trouble himself with the distinctions, attempted or alluded to, between Fancy and Imagination. The subject is jaded, the matter of it insignificant, and the settlement of it practically impossible, not merely because everybody has his own theory, but also because nobody ever states his own in terms on which other people are agreed. I am myself now entirely indifferent which word I use; and should say of a work of art that it was well 'fancied,' or well 'invented,' or well 'imagined,' with only some shades of different meaning in the application of the terms, rather dependent on the matter treated, than the power of mind involved in the treatment" (4:220). This change of heart, of course, comes nine years after the publication of Pater's essay.

20. "Unfortunately, the works of metaphysicians will afford us in this most interesting inquiry, no aid whatsoever" (4:224). Ruskin easily dismisses Dugald Stewart, for example, whose "meagre" definitions of imagination and fancy are "not only inefficient and obscure, but utterly inapplicable" (4:226).

21. Crawford suggests that Pater probably knew Tylor and the doctrine of survivals through his friend, the poet, translator, and anthropological theorist Andrew Lang: "There is no evidence that Pater read Tylor, but he did read Lang" (Crawford, 873). Inman believes, as I do, that "anyone who considers the internal evidence . . . will be persuaded that Pater read Tylor" (*Pater and His Reading*, x).

22. On the relation between Pater's and Hegel's idea of historical development, in addition to Shuter, see Dale; Williams; and McGrath (118–39). For an analysis of Pater's figural strategies of "revival," see Williams. Other images and ideas of rebirth in Pater include the Christian doctrine of resurrection and the nineteenth-century idea of the exile and return of the pagan gods who survived the triumph of Christianity by hiding themselves on earth.

23. In *Fors Clavigera* (1871–78), Ruskin describes Scott in terms that resemble his idea of the gentleman. Scott is born of the "purest Border race," Ruskin writes; he possesses a "universal" sympathy manifest in action, self-command when he needs it, and a conspicuous reserve (27:565). For a discussion of the pathetic fallacy in relation to Ruskin's idea of the gentleman see my essay, "Figures of Restraint: The Ruskinian Gentleman and the Romantic Artist" (1998).

24. According to Ruskin the following lines from Scott's *Rokeby* do not contain the pathetic fallacy, although the personification in the lines is obvious.

> And from the grassy slope he sees
> The Greta flow to meet the Tees;
> Where issuing from her darksome bed,
> She caught the morning's eastern red,
> And through the softening vale below
> Roll'd her bright waves in rosy glow,
> All blushing to her bridal bed,
> Like some shy maid, in convent bred;
> While linnet, lark, and blackbird gay
> Sing forth her nuptial roundelay.

Scott's metaphorical depiction of the Greta as a rosy blushing bride happily rolling to her bridal bed is, Ruskin emphasizes, "not *pathetic* fallacy, for there is no passion in *Scott* which alters nature" (5:341). Ruskin detects both sympathy and restraint in these lines, a profound apprehension of joy in the morning sun's soft reflection on the river's surface, despite the beholder's present unhappiness. "Is Scott, or are the persons of his story, gay at this moment?" Ruskin asks. "Far from it. Neither Scott nor Risingham is happy, but the Greta is; and all Scott's sympathy is ready for the Greta, on the instant" (5:341).

25. In the essay "Romanticism." I take this up again in chapter 4.

26. Arnold wrote of Wordsworth that "he had no style"; Coleridge had referred to his style as "matter-of-fact." Mill called Wordsworth "the poet of unpoetical natures," and Martineau wrote that "with all their truth and all their charm, few of Wordsworth's pieces are poems" (Ward, 64).

Chapter Two: Romanticism and the Italian Renaissance

1. Crowe and Cavalcaselle published their plodding three-volume *New History of Painting in Italy* from 1864 to 1866. Important studies were completed on the continent, especially Jules Michelet's *La Renaissance* of 1855, the seventh volume of his *Histoire de France*. Along with Edgar Quinet's *Les Revolutions d'Italie* of 1849, Michelet's study revised Renaissance historiography by challenging the assumptions of the French Catholic school and their religious condemnation of the Italian Renaissance. The most influential apology for Christian art, Alexis-François Rio's *de l'art chrétien* of 1836, was translated into English in 1854. Jacob Burckhardt's *Civilization of the Renaissance in Italy* was published in German in 1860. Strangely enough, there is no evidence that Pater ever read Burckhardt

(Inman, *Pater's Reading*, 221). The many important parallels between the Swiss historian's and Pater's conceptions of the Renaissance—its extreme individualism, religious skepticism, reconciliation of Christian and pagan elements, and ideal of cultural unity, what Pater calls *Allgemeinheit*—can most likely be traced to their common reading in Goethe and the German Romantics. John Addington Symonds's *The Age of the Despots*, the first volume of his seven-volume *Renaissance in Italy*, did not appear until 1875. Mrs. Mark Pattison's *Renaissance of Art in France* was published in 1879 and Vernon Lee's *Euphorion: being Studies of the Antique and the Medieval in the Renaissance*, which was dedicated to Pater, in 1884. See Hilary Fraser's *The Victorians and Renaissance Italy* for a recent account of the status of the Italian Renaissance in Victorian England. See also J. B. Bullen, *The Myth of the Renaissance in Nineteenth-Century Writing*.

2. Among Ruskin's endless classifications is his casuistical distinction between the true and the false grotesque, an argument that echoes the pathetic fallacy in its contrast between healthy and unhealthy romanticism.

3. All references to *The Renaissance* will be cited in the text by page number from *The Renaissance*, edited by Donald L. Hill.

4. In his conviction that an "outbreak" of the Renaissance spirit occurred within the Middle Age itself, Pater follows Michelet. As Inman explains, "According to Michelet, [in *La Renaissance*, Volume VII of the *Histoire de France*] . . . a number of abortive efforts of the human spirit challenged the medieval tyranny during the late Middle Ages" (*Pater's Reading*, 282–84). "Throughout the Middle Ages Michelet is impatient for the Renaissance," remarks Edmund Wilson (*To the Finland Station*, 12).

5. Donald Hill points out that the "phrase 'Christian art' had a vogue or currency" at the time, primarily due to the work of Rio and Lindsay, both favorites of Ruskin. Hill quotes Ruskin speaking in *Modern Painters V* of "the art which, since the writings of Rio and Lord Lindsay, is specially known as 'Christian.'" In 1872, only months before Pater composed his "Preface," Ruskin wrote an enthusiastic "Preface" to John Tyrwhitt's new book, *Christian Art and Symbolism*, a book with which Pater was most likely familiar (Hill, 300).

6. The survival of "a strange rival religion" manifest as a pagan element in art is more complex than even Pater indicates. See Jean Seznec's still valuable *Survival of the Pagan Gods*.

7. "Far more than Ruskin," writes Richard Stein, "Pater self-consciously develops an art of history, which involves new techniques for the analysis of the past and new standards for the sort of materials that characterize an epoch. The revolutionary quality of *The Renaissance* depends not merely on a reinterpretation of the meaning of a particular historic period but also on a reassessment of the nature of history itself" (224). See also Bullen, "The Historiography of *Studies in the History of the Renaissance*," 155–67.

8. From "Pre-Raphaelitism," Lecture VI of the *Lectures on Architecture and Painting*.

9. At this point in the essay, Pater is specifically referring to Newman's "partial" view of Greek religion, as expressed in *An Essay on the Development of Christian Doctrine* (Hill, 428). Later in the essay he will hint at Arnold's failure to recognize the sadness in the Greek religion, "Theocritus too, often strikes a note of romantic sadness" (47). In the 1864 "Pagan and Medieval Religious Sentiment" Arnold had pointed to Theocritus's fifteenth idyll as evidence that "the ideal, cheerful, sensuous pagan life is not sick or sorry" (3:222).

10. The frontispiece of *Modern Painters V* is an engraving of Ruskin's 1845 sketch of Angelico's *Annunciation* from the sacristy of Santa Maria Novella.

11. Ruskin notes a number of defects in the Madonna of the Triptych, a consequence of Angelico's inability to draw a life-size head. Her eyes have a "stony stare," the ear has been set too far back, the hair "too far off the brow." In other respects, however, the painting exemplifies the "purest modes of giving a conception of superhuman but still creature form" (4:318) that Ruskin outlined in *Modern Painters II*: purity of color, decoration of a generic and abstract character, symmetrical design, the quality of repose.

> The child *stands* upon the Virgin's knees, one hand raised in the usual attitude of benediction, the other holding a globe. The face looks straightforward, quiet, Jupiter-like, and very sublime, owing to the smallness of the features in proportion to the head, the eyes being placed at about three-sevenths of the whole height, leaving four-sevenths for the brow, and themselves only in length about one-sixth of the breadth of the face, half closed, giving a peculiar appearance of repose. The hair is short, golden, symmetrically curled, statuesque in its contour; the mouth tender and full of life: the red cross of the glory about the head of an intense ruby enamel, almost fire colour; the dress brown, with golden girdle. (12:236)

12. In his later lectures—*Ariadne Florentina, Val D'Arno, The Aesthetic and Mathematical Schools of Art in Florence*—Ruskin argues that the Florentine purist school—Carpaccio, Botticelli, Giotto—is the result of the Florentines' historical intimacy with the Greek spirit. The account of that intimacy is very complex and depends on an ethnological analysis in which the early Florentine painters—like Giotto—belong literally to a Greco-Etruscan race. Botticelli is a "reanimate" Greek, but a more noble "creature than the Greek who had died" (22:405) because he effects the ultimate reconciliation of Greek and Christian impulses, superseding in spiritual vitality the Venetian painters of "worldly harmony" (Fitch, 614–34).

13. As DeLaura points out, Pater "progressively eliminated" Hegel's name from revisions of the essay between 1867 and the third edition of *The Renaissance* in 1888 (*Hebrew and Hellene*, 211).

14. René Wellek suggests that Pater's Renaissance "actually ends with Goethe" ("Pater's Literary Theory," 35).

15. Winckelmann is, for Pater, a historically realized instance of the diaphanous ideal. See Francis Roellinger, "Intimations of Winckelmann in Pater's 'Diaphaneite.'"

Chapter Three: Leonardo, Michelangelo and the Oxford Lectures

1. Ruskin's enthusiasm upon accepting the appointment as Slade Professor was tempered with some apprehension and anxiety. His experience as a student at Christ Church had not been a particularly happy one—"I myself look upon the years I spent at Oxford as among the most disagreeable in my life," he wrote to his cousin George Richardson in 1860 (Birch, 132)—and his return elicited the same nervousness and antipathy toward academic competitiveness that he had felt as a young man. He was especially anxious about offending University authorities, and assured Henry Acland, his college friend and a staunch supporter of Ruskin's appointment, that he would be "surprised . . . at the generally quiet tone to which I shall reduce myself in all public duty" (20:xix–xxi.).

2. Austin argues that by his second tenure Ruskin was more willing to capitulate to popular taste. She traces a shift from the elitist, ambition-oriented rhetoric of the first tenure to the ratification of middle-class satisfaction in his second tenure, a result of his increasing appreciation of the "power of popular taste in the market" (34–43).

3. At least according to Swinburne. In a letter to John Morley, April 11, 1873, Swinburne recollects that "on my telling him [Pater] once at Oxford how highly Rossetti (D.G.) as well as myself estimated his first papers in the *Fortnightly*, he replied to the effect that he considered them as owing their inspiration entirely to the example of my own work in the same line" (*Letters*, 2:240–41).

4. Pater mentions Luini once, merely as one of many artists who "re-echoed" Leonardo's original conceptions.

5. See J. B. Bullen's "Walter Pater's Interpretation of the Mona Lisa as a Symbol of Romanticism" (139–52) for a discussion of Pater's interpretation of the Mona Lisa as "the quintessential expression of the Romantic spirit in art."

6. In the essay on Pico, Pater credits him for using the phrase before Bacon. "And in the midst of all is placed man, *nodus et vinculum mundi*, the bond or copula of the world, and the 'interpreter of nature': that famous expression of Bacon's really belongs to Pico" (*Renaissance*, 31).

7. In all the editions of *The Renaissance*, Pater describes Leonardo's paintings as conveying "pathetic power" rather than "tenderness," the original description in the 1869 *Fortnightly* essay.

8. In his appendix to *Modern Painters IV*, "Modern Grotesque," Ruskin laments Leonardo's constant indulgence in "caricature and exaggeration." He stresses, however, that this caricature "consists, not in imperfect or violent *drawing*, but in delicate and perfect drawing of strange and exaggerated forms quaintly combined." But Ruskin finds this habit "injurious; I strongly suspect its operation on Leonardo to have been the increase of his non-natural tendencies in his higher works" (6:470).

9. *Academy* 4 (March 15, 1873): 105. Quoted in Hill, 343.

10. Inman agrees, speculating that Pater, "under the impetus of Ruskin's lecture," put aside his work on Abelard and du Bellay in order to compose or complete the essay on Michelangelo (*Pater's Reading*, 246). See J. B. Bullen, "Pater and Ruskin on Michelangelo: Two Contrasting Views," for an excellent account of the two critics' "different view[s] of Michelangelo" (56).

11. In England, this tradition runs from Jonathan Richardson and Sir Joshua Reynolds, through John Opie and Henry Fuseli, and into the nineteenth century, including William Wordsworth, Michael Scott, and Lord Lindsay. In France, the emphasis upon Michelangelo's power was even more pervasive, with Stendhal, Delacroix, Baudelaire, Quinet, Michelet, and Taine all contributing to this view of the artist (Bullen, "Pater and Ruskin," 57–60).

12. "The Northern temper," declares Ruskin, "accepts the scholarship of the Reformation with absolute sincerity, while the Italians seek refuge from it in the partly scientific and completely lascivious enthusiasms of literature and painting, renewed under classical influence" (22:80–81).

13. Especially the work of J. C. Robinson and Charles C. Perkins in the 1850s and 1860s (Bullen, "Pater and Ruskin," 60).

14. "Prelude to Michelangelo" was the original title for the never published Arezzo manuscript. Inman suggests that it was composed at the same time as the comments on Luca and was to be combined with it. For another hypothesis about the composition of "Arezzo," see Laurel Brake, "A Commentary on 'Arezzo': an Unpublished Manuscript by Walter Pater." Inman suggests that after Pater dropped "Arezzo" he also changed the title from "Prelude to Michelangelo" to "Luca della Robbia" because he wanted to emphasize the value of della Robbia's art in itself. The essay begins with the statement, "The Italian sculptors of the earlier half of the fifteenth century are more than mere forerunners of the great masters of its close. . . ." Pater's analysis of Michelangelo, however, still makes up at least half of the essay.

15. See Lecture VI of *Aratra Pentilici*, "The School of Athens" (20:331–54).

Chapter Four: Romanticism and the Oxford Lectures

1. In the course of the second lecture, Ruskin pauses to explain how he characterizes the Pre-Raphaelite school as both "obstinately realistic" and "romantic." Realism and romance are not opposed, he argues.

> [R]omance does not consist in the manner of representing or relating things, but in the kind of passions appealed to by the things related. The three romantic passions are those by which you are told, in Wordsworth's aphoristic line, that the life of the soul is fed:
> "We live by Admiration, Hope, and Love." (33:292)

We saw in Chapter 1 that Ruskin often reverted to the line, believing that it represented "the teaching and main dividing of all that I have . . . written." The point is similar to that he makes in the last lecture of the series, "The Hillside," where he stresses that he does "not use the word Romantic as opposed to Classic, but as opposed to the prosaic characters of selfishness and stupidity, in all times, and among all nations" (33:374).

2. This suggestion is made by Christian W. Willerton in chapter 8 of his dissertation, "A Study of Walter Pater's *Appreciations*." Willerton makes a detailed comparison of the two essays.

3. See James Eli Adams's *Dandies and Desert Saints* for an extended discussion of restraint in Pater. Adams describes Pater's appeal to discipline as an attempt "to reinscribe within the ethos of aestheticism familiar norms of Victorian masculinity, and thereby to present even spectatorship as an eminently virile self-discipline" (150).

4. For an analysis of Ruskin's *Fiction, Fair and Foul* and his critique of modern fiction's "urban aesthetic" see Austin, *The Practical Ruskin* (131–68).

5. As John J. Conlon writes, "By far the most influential writer and critic who opened the multifaceted world of French culture to his countrymen and whose works and disciples altered the course of English literature in that regard was Walter Pater" ("Reception of French Literature," 34–46). See also Conlon's *Walter Pater and the French Tradition*.

6. At least one contemporary reviewer remarked that Pater has been contaminated by French influence. "It is rather terrible," grumbles Mrs. Oliphant in her review of *Appreciations*, "to meet with this old classical and romantic business in the discussion of English literature. We have had, Heaven knows, enough of it in French to bewilder anybody's brain, and a new definition is more than human nature can support, especially where it makes nothing clear, and is not wanted in a language like ours. . . . [W]e must protest, on our side, against a

152NOTES TO PAGES 129–137

foreign model which is altogether out of the question as affording any rule for us," and she concludes that "Mr. Pater's French standard leads him away from the natural English censors." From her unsigned review, *Blackwood's Magazine*, January 1890. Quoted in Seiler, 218.

7. For a discussion of Mill's influence on Pater, see Timothy Weiss, "Walter Pater, Aesthetic Utilitarian": "Pater aspires to combine a special appreciation of art, music, literature, and philosophy, with a social consciousness, as does Mill in his influential essay, 'Utilitarianism' " (105).

Conclusion

1. I am summarizing Jerome McGann's description of Wordsworth's "Intimations Ode": "The poem annihilates its history, biographical and sociohistorical alike, and replaces these particulars with a record of pure consciousness" (90).

2. In his book *Romantic Ecology*, Jonathan Bate responds to the critique of romantic ideology by repoliticizing romanticism, turning away from McGann's broadly Marxist position in favor of an ecological viewpoint. Ruskin is a cornerstone of his rescue efforts: "I propose that the Romantic Ideology is not, as Jerome McGann has it, a theory of imagination and symbol embodied in such self-consciously idealist and elitist texts as Coleridge's *Statesman's Manual*, but a theory of ecosystems and unalienated labour embodied in such self-consciously pragmatic and populist texts as Ruskin's *Fors Clavigera*" (10). That Ruskin can be read as consistent with both new historicist and ecological theories is evidence of his ambivalent relation to romanticism, which I have traced throughout my study.

3. In the later version of the essay, Pater describes the "aesthetic poetry," of which Morris is the "first typical specimen," as "an afterthought" of the romantic school.

4. While there is general agreement that Pater amended his youthful apostasy, readers disagree as to the extent of the shift in Pater's religious thought. Most recently, William Shuter suggests that later in his life, despite never explicitly renouncing his earlier views or acknowledging any change in his religious position, Pater "undertook the office of Christian apologist" (*Rereading Pater*, 52).

Works Cited

Abrams, M. H. "Two Roads to Wordsworth." In *Wordsworth: A Collection of Critical Essays*, edited by M. H. Abrams. Englewood Cliffs, N.J.: Prentice Hall, 1972.

Adams, James Eli. *Dandies and Desert Saints: Styles of Victorian Masculinity*. Ithaca, N.Y.: Cornell University Press, 1995.

Alcoff, Linda. "Cultural Feminism versus Post-Structuralism: The Identity Crisis in Feminist Theory." *Signs* 13 (spring 1988): 405–36.

Arac, Jonathan. *Critical Genealogies: Historical Situations for Postmodern Literary Studies*. New York: Columbia University Press, 1987.

Arnold, Matthew. *The Complete Prose Works of Matthew Arnold*. Edited by R. H. Super. 11 vols. Ann Arbor: University of Michigan Press, 1960–77.

Aske, Martin. *Keats and Hellenism: An Essay*. Cambridge: Cambridge University Press, 1985.

Austin, Linda. *The Practical Ruskin: Economics and Audience in the Late Work*. Baltimore: Johns Hopkins University Press, 1991.

Babbitt, Irving. *Rousseau and Romanticism*. Boston: Houghton Mifflin, 1919.

Barzun, Jacques. "To the Rescue of Romanticism." *American Scholar* (spring 1940): 147–58.

Bate, Jonathan. *Romantic Ecology: Wordsworth and the Environmental Tradition*. London: Routledge, 1991.

Beer, John, ed. *Questioning Romanticism*. Baltimore: Johns Hopkins University Press, 1995.

Benson, A. C. *Walter Pater*. London: Macmillan and Co., 1906.

Birch, Dinah. *Ruskin's Myths*. Oxford: Clarendon Press, 1988.

Bizup, Joseph. "Walter Pater and the Ruskinian Gentleman." *English Literature in Transition* 38, no. 1 (1995): 51–69.

Bloom, Harold. "Introduction." In *The Literary Criticism of John Ruskin*, edited by Harold Bloom. New York: Da Capo Press, 1965.

————. "The Place of Pater: Marius the Epicurean." In *The Ringers in the Tower: Studies in Romantic Tradition*, 185–96. Chicago: University of Chicago Press, 1971.

————. "The Crystal Man." In *Selected Writings of Walter Pater*, edited by Harold Bloom, vii–xxxi. New York: Columbia University Press, 1974.

Bourke, Richard. *Romantic Discourse and Political Modernity: Wordsworth, the Intellectual and Cultural Critique*. New York: Harvester Wheatsheaf, 1993.

Brake, Laurel. "A Commentary on 'Arezzo': An Unpublished Manuscript by Walter Pater." *Review of English Studies* 27 (August 1976): 273–76.

————. *Walter Pater*. Plymouth, U.K.: Northcote House Publishers, 1994.

————. "After Studies: Walter Pater's Cancelled Book, or Dionysus and Gay Discourse in the 1870s." In *Beauty and the Beast: Christina Rossetti, Walter Pater, R. L. Stevenson and Their Contemporaries*, edited by Peter Liebregts and Wim Tigges. Amsterdam: Rodopi, 1996.

Buchanan, Robert. *The Fleshly School of Poetry*. London: Strahan, 1872.

Buckler, William. *Walter Pater: The Critic as Artist of Ideas*. New York: New York University Press, 1987.

Bullen, Barrie. "Walter Pater's 'Renaissance' and Leonardo Da Vinci's Reputation in the Nineteenth Century." *Modern Language Review* 74 (April 1979): 268–80.

Bullen, J. B. "Pater and Ruskin on Michelangelo: Two Contrasting Views." In *Walter Pater: An Imaginary Sense of Fact*, edited by Philip Dodd. London: Frank Cass and Co., 1981.

————. "Walter Pater's Interpretation of the Mona Lisa as a Symbol of Romanticism." In *The Romantic Heritage*, edited by Karsten Engelberg. Copenhagen: Publications of the Department of English, University of Copenhagen, 1983.

————. "The Historiography of *Studies in the History of the Renaissance*." In *Pater in the 1990s*, edited by Laurel Brake and Ian Small. Greensboro, N.C.: ELT Press, 1991.

————. *The Myth of the Renaissance in Nineteenth-Century Writing*. Oxford: Clarendon Press, 1994.

Burne-Jones, Giorgiana. *Memorials of Edward Burne-Jones*. 2 vols. London: Macmillan, 1909.

Butler, Marilyn. *Romantics, Rebels and Reactionaries: English Literature and Its Background, 1760–1830*. Oxford: Oxford University Press, 1981.

Carrier, David. "Baudelaire, Pater and the Origins of Modernism." *Comparative Criticism* 17 (1995): 109–22.

Christ, Carol T. *Victorian and Modern Poetics*. Chicago: University of Chicago Press, 1984.

Claiborne, Jay Wood. "Two Secretaries: The Letters of John Ruskin to Charles Augustus Howell and Rev. Richard St. John Tyrwhitt." Ph.D. diss., University of Texas, 1969.

Clark, Kenneth. *Ruskin at Oxford*. Oxford: Clarendon Press, 1947.

———. "Introduction." In *The Renaissance*, by Walter Pater. Cleveland: World Publishers Co., 1961.

Clayton, Jay, and Eric Rothstein, eds. *Influence and Intertextuality in Literary History*. Madison: University of Wisconsin Press, 1991.

Clements, Patricia. *Baudelaire and the English Tradition*. Princeton, N.J.: Princeton University Press, 1985.

Collingwood, W. G. *The Life of John Ruskin*. Boston: Houghton Mifflin, 1902.

Conlon, John J. *Walter Pater and the French Tradition*. Lewisburg, Pa.: Bucknell University Press, 1982.

———. "The Reception of French Literature in England, 1885–1914." In *Studies in Anglo-French Cultural Relations: Imagining France*, edited by Ceri Crossley and Ian Small. Houndmills, U.K.: Macmillan Press, 1988.

Connor, Steven. "Myth as Multiplicity in Walter Pater's Greek Studies and 'Denys L'Auxerrois.'" *Review of English Studies* 34 (1983): 28–42.

[Courthope, W. J.] "The State of English Poetry." *Quarterly Review* 135 (July 1873): 140.

———. "Modern Culture." *Quarterly Review* 137 (1874): 389–415.

———. "Wordsworth and Gray." *Quarterly Review* 141 (1876): 104–36.

Courthope, W. J. *The Liberal Movement in English Literature*. London: John Murray, 1885.

Crawford, Robert. "Pater's *Renaissance*, Andrew Lang, and Anthropological Romanticism." *English Literary History* 53 (winter 1986): 849–79.

Dale, Peter Allan. *The Victorian Critic and the Idea of History: Carlyle, Arnold, Pater*. Cambridge: Harvard University Press, 1977.

Daley, Kenneth. "From the Theoretic to the Practical: Ruskin, British Aestheticism, and the Relation of Art to Use." *Prose Studies* 20, no. 2 (August 1997): 90–107.

———. "Figures of Restraint: The Ruskinian Gentleman and the Romantic Artist." *The Victorian Newsletter* (spring 1998): 10–13.

Decker, Clarence R. *The Victorian Conscience*. New York: Twayne Publishers, 1952.

DeLaura, David. "The 'Wordsworth' of Pater and Arnold: 'The Supreme Artistic View of Life.'" *Studies in English Literature 1500–1900* 6, no. 4 (autumn 1966): 651–67.

———. *Hebrew and Hellene in Victorian England: Newman, Arnold, and Pater*. Austin: University of Texas Press, 1969.

————. "The Revaluation of 'Christian' Art: Ruskin's Appreciation of Fra Angelico, 1845–60." *University of Toronto Quarterly: A Canadian Journal of the Humanities* 43 (1974): 143–50.

Dellamora, Richard. *Masculine Desire: The Sexual Politics of Victorian Aestheticism.* Chapel Hill: University of North Carolina Press, 1990.

de Man, Paul. "Wordsworth and the Victorians." In *The Rhetoric of Romanticism,* 83–92. New York: Columbia University Press, 1984.

Donoghue, Denis. *Walter Pater: Lover of Strange Souls.* New York: Alfred A. Knopf, 1995.

Dowling, Linda. *Hellenism and Homosexuality in Victorian Oxford.* Ithaca, N.Y.: Cornell University Press, 1994.

————. *The Vulgarization of Art: The Victorians and Aesthetic Democracy.* Charlottesville: University Press of Virginia, 1996.

Elfenbein, Andrew. *Byron and the Victorians.* Cambridge: Cambridge University Press, 1995.

Ellmann, Richard. "The Critic as Artist as Wilde." In *The Artist as Critic: Critical Writings of Oscar Wilde,* edited by Richard Ellmann. Chicago: University of Chicago Press, 1968.

————. "Overtures to 'Salome.'" In *Oscar Wilde,* edited by Harold Bloom. New York: Chelsea House, 1985.

————. *Oscar Wilde.* New York: Vintage Books, 1987.

Fellows, Jay. *Tombs, Despoiled and Haunted: "Under-Textures" and "After-Thoughts" in Walter Pater.* Stanford, Calif.: Stanford University Press, 1991.

Finley, C. Stephen. *Nature's Covenant: Figures of Landscape in Ruskin.* University Park: The Pennsylvania State University Press, 1992.

Fishman, Solomon. *The Interpretation of Art: Essays on the Art Criticism of John Ruskin, Walter Pater, Clive Bell, Roger Fry, and Herbert Read.* Berkeley: University of California Press, 1963.

Fitch, Raymond E. *The Poison Sky: Myth and Apocalypse in Ruskin.* Athens: Ohio University Press, 1982.

Foucault, Michel. "What Is an Author?" In *Language, Counter-Memory, Practice: Selected Essays and Interviews by Michel Foucault,* edited by Donald F. Bouchard. Ithaca, N.Y.: Cornell University Press, 1977.

Fraser, Hilary. *The Victorians and Renaissance Italy.* Oxford: Blackwell, 1992.

Friedman, Susan Stanford. "Weavings: Intertextuality and the (Re)Birth of the Author." In *Influence and Intertextuality in Literary History,* edited by Jay Clayton and Eric Rothstein. Madison: University of Wisconsin Press, 1991.

Galperin, William. *Revision and Authority in Wordsworth: The Interpretation of a Career.* Philadelphia: University of Pennsylvania Press, 1989.

Gill, Stephen. *Wordsworth and the Victorians.* Oxford: Clarendon Press, 1998.

Gurewitsch, Susan. "Golgonooza on the Grand Canal: Ruskin's *Stones of Venice* and the Romantic Imagination." *The Arnoldian* 9, no. 1 (winter 1981): 25–39.

Harris, Wendell V. *The Omnipresent Debate: Empiricism and Transcendentalism in Nineteenth-Century English Prose.* DeKalb: Northern Illinois University Press, 1981.

————. "Ruskin and Pater—Hebrew and Hellene—Explore the Renaissance." *CLIO* 17, no. 2 (1988): 173–85.

Harrison, Antony H. *Victorian Poets and Romantic Poems: Intertextuality and Ideology.* Charlottesville: University Press of Virginia, 1990.

Hassan, Ihab. "Toward a Concept of Postmodernism." In *Postmodernism: A Reader,* edited by Thomas Docherty. New York: Columbia University Press, 1993.

Helsinger, Elizabeth. *Ruskin and the Art of the Beholder.* Cambridge: Harvard University Press, 1982.

Hickey, Alison. *Impure Conceits: Rhetoric and Ideology in Wordsworth's "Excursion."* Stanford, Calif.: Stanford University Press, 1997.

Hill, Donald, ed. *The Renaissance,* by Walter Pater. Berkeley: University of California Press, 1980.

Hilton, Tim. "Road Digging and Aestheticism, Oxford 1875." *Studio International* 188 (December 1974): 226–29.

Homans, Margaret. *Bearing the Word: Language and Female Experience in Nineteenth-Century Women Writers.* New Haven, Conn.: Yale University Press, 1986.

Hough, Graham. *The Last Romantics.* London: Gerald Duckworth, 1949.

Houghton, Walter E. *The Victorian Frame of Mind 1830–1870.* New Haven, Conn.: Yale University Press, 1957.

Inman, Billie Andrew. *Walter Pater's Reading: A Bibliography of His Library Borrowings and Literary References, 1858–1873.* New York: Garland Publishing, 1981.

————. *Walter Pater and His Reading 1874–1877: With a Bibliography of His Library Borrowings, 1878–1894.* New York: Garland Publishing, 1990.

Iser, Wolfgang. *Walter Pater: The Aesthetic Moment.* Translated by David Henry Wilson. Cambridge: Cambridge University Press, 1987.

Jenkyns, Richard. *The Victorians and Ancient Greece.* Cambridge: Harvard University Press, 1980.

Johnson, Lee McKay. *The Metaphor of Painting: Essays on Baudelaire, Ruskin, Proust, and Pater.* Ann Arbor: UMI Research Press, 1980.

Johnson, R. V. "Pater and the Victorian Anti-Romantics." *Essays in Criticism* 4 (1954): 42–57.

Keefe, Robert, and Janice A. Keefe. *Walter Pater and the Gods of Disorder.* Athens: Ohio University Press, 1988.

Kermode, Frank. *The Romantic Image.* New York: Vintage Books, 1957.

Kissane, James. "Victorian Mythology." *Victorian Studies* 6 (1962): 5–28.

Kitchin, G. W. *Ruskin in Oxford, and Other Stories*. London: Murray, 1904.

Knoepflmacher, U. C. "Dover Revisited: The Wordsworthian Matrix in the Poetry of Matthew Arnold." *Victorian Poetry* 1 (1963): 17–26.

——. "Mutations of the Wordsworthian Child of Nature." In *Nature and the Victorian Imagination*, edited by U. C. Knoepflmacher and G. B. Tennyson. Berkeley: University of California Press, 1977.

——. "Arnold's Fancy and Pater's Imagination: Exclusion and Incorporation." *Victorian Poetry* 26, nos. 1–2 (1988): 103–15.

Kramer, Lawrence. "The 'Intimations' Ode and Victorian Romanticism." *Victorian Poetry* 18, no. 4 (winter 1980): 315–36.

Leng, Andrew. "Pater's Aesthetic Poet: The Appropriation of Rossetti from Ruskin." *The Journal of Pre-Raphaelite and Aesthetic Studies* 2, no. 1 (spring 1989): 42–48.

Levey, Michael. "Botticelli and Nineteenth-Century England." *Journal of the Warburg and Courtauld Institutes* 23 (1960): 291–306.

Lindenberger, Herbert. *The History in Literature: On Value, Genre, Institutions*. New York: Columbia University Press, 1990.

Livingston, Ira. *Arrow of Chaos: Romanticism and Postmodernity*. Minneapolis: University of Minnesota Press, 1997.

Loesberg, Jonathan. *Aestheticism and Deconstruction: Pater, Derrida, and De Man*. Princeton, N.J.: Princeton University Press, 1991.

Logan, James Venable. *Wordsworthian Criticism: A Guide and Bibliography*. Columbus: Ohio State University Press, 1947.

Lovejoy, A. O. "On the Discrimination of Romanticisms." *PMLA* 39 (1924): 229–53.

McGann, Jerome J. *The Romantic Ideology: A Critical Investigation*. Chicago: University of Chicago Press, 1983.

McGrath, F. C. *The Sensible Spirit: Walter Pater and the Modernist Paradigm*. Tampa: University of South Florida Press, 1986.

Meisel, Perry. *The Absent Father: Virginia Woolf and Walter Pater*. New Haven, Conn.: Yale University Press, 1980.

——. *The Myth of the Modern: A Study in British Literature and Criticism after 1850*. New Haven, Conn.: Yale University Press, 1987.

Miller, Nancy K. *Subject to Change: Reading Feminist Writing*. New York: Columbia University Press, 1988.

Monsman, Gerald. "Pater and His Younger Contemporaries." *The Victorian Newsletter* 48 (1975): 1–9.

——. *Walter Pater*. Boston: Twayne Publishers, 1977.

Morgan, Thaïs E. "Rereading Nature: Wordsworth between Swinburne and

Arnold." *Victorian Poetry* 24, no. 4 (winter 1986): 427–39.

———. "Reimagining Masculinity in Victorian Criticism: Swinburne and Pater." *Victorian Studies* 36, no. 3 (spring 1993): 315–32.

Morley, John. "Introduction." In *The Complete Poetical Works of William Wordsworth*, edited by John Morley. London: Macmillan and Co., 1888.

Nevinson, Henry. *Changes and Chances*. New York: Harcourt, Brace and Co., 1924.

O'Hara, Daniel T. *The Romance of Interpretation: Visionary Criticism from Pater to de Man*. New York: Columbia University Press, 1985.

Parker, Mark. "Measure and Countermeasure: The Lovejoy-Wellek Debate and Romantic Periodization." In *Theoretical Issues in Literary Theory*, edited by David Perkins. Cambridge: Harvard University Press, 1991.

Pater, Walter. "Coleridge's Writings." *Westminster Review* 85 (January–April 1866): 48–60.

———. "Winckelmann." *Westminster Review* 87 (January–April 1867): 36–50.

———. "Poems by William Morris." *Westminster Review* 90 (July–October 1868): 144–49.

———. "Notes on Leonardo Da Vinci." *Fortnightly Review* 6 (November 1869): 494–508.

———. "The Poetry of Michelangelo." *Fortnightly Review* 16 (November 1871): 559–70.

———. "On Wordsworth." *Fortnightly Review* 21 (April 1874): 455–65.

———. "Romanticism." *Macmillan's Magazine* 35 (November 1876): 64–70.

———. "Review of Ernest Chesneau's *The School of English Painting*." *The Oxford Magazine*, 25 February 1885.

———. *Appreciations*. London: Macmillan and Co., 1910.

———. *Imaginary Portraits*. London: Macmillan and Co., 1910.

———. *Plato and Platonism: A Series of Lectures*. London: Macmillan and Co., 1910.

———. *Letters of Walter Pater*. Edited by Lawrence Evans. Oxford: Oxford University Press, 1970.

———. *The Renaissance*. Edited by Donald L. Hill. Berkeley: University of California Press, 1980.

Perkins, David. *Is Literary History Possible?* Baltimore: Johns Hopkins University Press, 1992.

Poovey, Mary. "Feminism and Deconstruction." *Feminist Studies* 14 (spring 1988): 51–66.

Prettejohn, Elizabeth. "Walter Pater and Aesthetic Painting." In *After the Pre-Raphaelites: Art and Aestheticism in Victorian England*, edited by Elizabeth Prettejohn. New Brunswick, N.J.: Rutgers University Press, 1999.

Prickett, Stephen. *Romanticism and Religion: The Tradition of Coleridge and*

Wordsworth in the Victorian Church. Cambridge: Cambridge University Press, 1976.

Proust, Marcel. *On Reading Ruskin: Prefaces to "La Bible d'Amiens" and "Sesame et les Lys" with Selections from the Notes to the Translated Texts.* Translated and edited by Jean Autret, William Burford, and Philip J. Wolfe. New Haven, Conn.: Yale University Press, 1987.

Ricks, Christopher. *The Force of Poetry.* Oxford: Clarendon Press, 1984.

Riede, David. *Swinburne: A Study of Romantic Mythmaking.* Charlottesville: University Press of Virginia, 1978.

———. *Matthew Arnold and the Betrayal of Language.* Charlottesville: University Press of Virginia, 1988.

Roellinger, Francis. "Intimations of Winckelmann in Pater's 'Diaphaneitè.'" *English Language Notes* 2, no. 4 (1965): 277–82.

Ruskin, John. *The Works of John Ruskin.* Edited by E. T. Cook and Alexander Wedderburn. 39 vols. London: George Allen, 1903–12.

———. *Ruskin's Letters from Venice, 1851–1852.* Edited by John Lewis Bradley. New Haven, Conn.: Yale University Press, 1955.

———. *Ruskin in Italy: Letters to His Parents 1845.* Edited by Harold I. Shapiro. Oxford: Clarendon Press, 1972.

Sawyer, Paul. *Ruskin's Poetic Argument: The Design of the Major Works.* Ithaca, N.Y.: Cornell University Press, 1985.

Sayre, Robert, and Michael Lowy. "Figures of Romantic Anticapitalism." In *Spirits of Fire: English Romantic Writers and Contemporary Historical Methods,* edited by G. A. Rosso and Daniel P. Watkins. Rutherford, N.J.: Fairleigh Dickinson University Press, 1990.

Seiler, R. M., ed. *Walter Pater: The Critical Heritage.* London: Routledge and Kegan Paul, 1980.

Seznec, Jean. *The Survival of the Pagan Gods: The Mythological Tradition and Its Place in Renaissance Humanism and Art.* New York: Pantheon Books, 1953.

Sharp, William. "Personal Reminiscences of Walter Pater." In *Papers Critical and Reminiscent,* edited by Mrs. William Sharp. London: Heinemann, 1912.

Shuter, William F. "History as Palingenesis in Pater and Hegel." *PMLA* 86 (May 1971): 411–21.

———. *Rereading Walter Pater.* Cambridge: Cambridge University Press, 1997.

Siskin, Clifford. *The Historicity of Romantic Discourse.* New York: Oxford University Press, 1988.

Spear, Jeffrey. *Dreams of an English Eden: Ruskin and His Tradition in Social Criticism.* New York: Columbia University Press, 1984.

Sprinker, Michael. "Ruskin on the Imagination." *Studies in Romanticism* 18 (spring 1979): 115–39.

————. *Imaginary Relations: Aesthetics and Ideology in the Theory of Historical Materialism.* London: Verso, 1987.

Stange, G. Robert. "Art Criticism as a Prose Genre." In *The Art of Victorian Prose*, edited by George Levine and William Madden. New York: Oxford University Press, 1968.

Stein, Richard. *The Ritual of Interpretation: The Fine Arts as Literature in Ruskin, Rossetti, and Pater.* Cambridge: Harvard University Press, 1975.

Stoddart, Judith. *Ruskin's Culture Wars: Fors Clavigera and the Crisis of Victorian Liberalism.* Charlottesville: University Press of Virginia, 1998.

Swinburne, Algernon Charles. *The Complete Works of Algernon Charles Swinburne.* Edited by Sir Edmund Gosse and Thomas J. Wise. 20 vols. London: William Heineman, 1926.

————. *Letters.* Edited by Cecil Y. Lang. 6 vols. New Haven, Conn.: Yale University Press, 1959–62.

Symonds, John Addington. *The Life of Michelangelo Buonarroti.* 2 vols. London: Macmillan and Co., 1911.

Tennyson, Alfred. *The Poems of Tennyson.* Edited by Christopher Ricks. 3 vols. Berkeley: University of California Press, 1987.

Timko, Michael. "Wordsworth's 'Ode' and Arnold's 'Dover Beach': Celestial Light and Confused Alarms." *Cithara* 13, no. 1 (1973): 53–63.

Tucker, Herbert F. *Tennyson and the Doom of Romanticism.* Cambridge: Harvard University Press, 1988.

Turner, Frank M. *The Greek Heritage in Victorian Britain.* New Haven, Conn.: Yale University Press, 1981.

Tylor, Edward. *Primitive Culture: Researches into the Development of Mythology, Philosophy, Religion, Language, Art, and Custom.* 2 vols. London: John Murray, 1871.

Viereck, Peter. *Metapolitics: From the Romantics to Hitler.* New York: Alfred A. Knopf, 1941.

Ward, J. P. "An Anxiety of No Influence." In *Pater in the 1990s*, edited by Laurel Brake and Ian Small. Greensboro, N.C.: ELT Press, 1991.

Weisinger, Herbert. "English Treatment of the Classical-Romantic Problem." *Modern Language Quarterly* 7 (1946): 477–88.

Weiss, Timothy. "Walter Pater, Aesthetic Utilitarian." *Victorians Institute Journal* 15 (1987):105–21.

Wellek, René. "Periods and Movements in Literary History." In *English Institute Annual 1940.* New York: Columbia University Press, 1941.

————. "The Concept of Romanticism in Literary History." *Comparative Literature* 1 (1949): 1–23, 147–72.

————. "Walter Pater's Literary Theory and Criticism." *Victorian Studies* 1, no. 1 (1957): 29–46.

Whalley, George. "England/ Romantic–Romanticism." In *"Romantic" and Its Cognates: The European History of a Word*, edited by Hans Eichner. Toronto: University of Toronto Press, 1972.

Wheeler, Michael. *Ruskin's God*. Cambridge: Cambridge University Press, 1999.

Wihl, Gary. *Ruskin and the Rhetoric of Infallibility*. New Haven, Conn.: Yale University Press, 1985.

Wilde, Oscar. "The Grosvenor Gallery." *Dublin University Magazine*, July 1877.

Willerton, Christian. "A Study of Walter Pater's *Appreciations*." Ph.D. diss., University of North Carolina at Chapel Hill, 1979.

Williams, Carolyn. *Transfigured World: Walter Pater's Aesthetic Historicism*. Ithaca, N.Y.: Cornell University Press, 1989.

Wilson, Edmund. *To the Finland Station: A Study in the Writing and Acting of History*. New York: Farrar, Straus and Giroux, 1972.

Wolfson, Susan. *The Questioning Presence: Wordsworth, Keats, and the Interrogative Mode in Romantic Poetry*. Ithaca, N.Y.: Cornell University Press, 1986.

Woodring, Carl. "Wordsworth and the Victorians." In *The Age of William Wordsworth: Critical Essays on the Romantic Tradition*, edited by Kenneth R. Johnston and Gene W. Ruoff. New Brunswick, N.J.: Rutgers University Press, 1987.

Wordsworth, William. *William Wordsworth: The Poems*. Edited by John O. Hayden. 2 vols. New Haven, Conn.: Yale University Press, 1981.

Yeats, William Butler. *The Autobiography of William Butler Yeats*. New York: Collier Books, 1965.

Index

and romantic/romanticism, 2–3,
    6–7, 15, 16, 18, 54–55, 115, 116, 119–23,
    126–27, 130, 131, 132, 133–34, 147 n.2,
    151 n.1, 152 n.2
and Rossetti, 115–18
and St. George's Guild, 88, 89
and Victorian liberalism, 139 n.4
and Wordsworth, 15, 17–23, 26–30,
    35–36, 40–41, 43–45, 100, 105, 110,
    122, 143 n.4, 151 n.1
Works:
*The Aesthetic and Mathematical Schools of
    Art in Florence,* 148 n.12
Aratra Pentelici, 91–92, 113–14, 150 n.15
Ariadne Florentina, 10, 88, 148 n.12
The Art of England, 7, 18, 116–18, 151 n.1
The Bible of Amiens, 9
The Eagle's Nest, 79
Fiction, Fair and Foul, 19, 29–30, 127, 151
    n.4
Fors Clavigera, 88, 89, 145 n.23, 152 n.2
"Franchise," 16, 55, 115, 118–23, 129
The Lectures on Architecture and Painting,
    7, 18, 66
Lectures on Art, 69, 76, 79, 88, 89–91,
    100–101
Modern Painters I, 19, 100
Modern Painters II, 10, 26–29, 34–35, 62,
    63, 71, 73, 76, 144 n.14, 145 n.19, 145
    n.20, 148 n.11
Modern Painters III, 7, 19, 22, 23, 35–37,
    39–43, 69, 71, 80, 103, 116, 122, 146
    n.24
Modern Painters IV, 150 n.8
Modern Painters V, 65, 69, 71, 72, 147 n.5,
    148 n.10
"The Nature of Gothic," 6–7
Praeterita, 1, 29
The Queen of the Air, 76, 95–96, 142 n.22
"The Relation between Michael An-
    gelo and Tintoret," 103–5, 106, 108,
    109–10, 113, 150 n.12
"A Review of Lord Lindsay's Sketches
    of the History of Christian Art," 73–75,

148 n.11
The Seven Lamps of Architecture, 8, 141
    n.13
The Stones of Venice, 7, 15, 51, 54–58, 62,
    63, 65, 66, 90, 94, 95, 100
The Three Colours of Pre-Raphaelitism, 116
Time and Tide, 89
Val D'Arno, 7, 115, 118–19, 148 n.12
Rutherford, Mark, 143 n.5

Sainte-Beuve, Charles Augustin, 141 n.15
Savanarola, Fra Girolamo, 108
Sawyer, Paul, 54
Sayre, Robert, and Michael Lowy, 3, 140
    n.7
Schelling, Friedrich Wilhelm Joseph, 38
Schiller, Friedrich, 68, 142 n.22
Schlegel, Friedrich and A. W., 4
Scott, Michael, 150 n.11
Scott, Sir Walter, 17, 19, 29, 30, 35, 40,
    42–44, 122–23, 125, 127, 140 n.8, 145
    n.23, 146 n.24
Seiler, R. M., 136, 151 n.6
Seznec, Jean, 147 n.6
Sharp, William, 141 n.16
Shelley, Percy Bysshe, 38, 43, 100
Shuter, William, 2, 39, 46, 139 n.2, 152 n.4
Signorelli, Luca, 108
Siskin, Clifford, 3
Spear, Jeffrey, 143 n.3
Spielmann, M. H., 88
Sprinker, Michael, 141 n.13
Stange, G. Robert, 142 n.19
Stein, Richard, 11, 60, 147 n.7
Stendhal, 130, 150 n.11
Stephens, Leslie, 32
Stewart, Dugald, 145 n.20
Swinburne, Algernon Charles, 8, 26, 52,
    76, 94, 127, 138, 144 n.13, 149 n.3
Symonds, John Addington, 79, 103–4, 146
    n.1

Taine, Hippolyte, 150 n.11
Tate, Allen, 134